THE

BECKET
LIST

C000068579

THE
BECKET LIST
An A to Z of First World Problems

HENRY BECKET

ILLUSTRATED BY TONY HUSBAND

Red Door

Dedicated to all those second-rate designers, manufacturers, managers, broadcasters, officials, writers, fellow travellers and suchlike who so selflessly and unintentionally have provided such rich source material

Published by RedDoor
www.reddoorpress.co.uk

Text © 2020 Henry Becket
Illustrations © 2020 Tony Husband

The right of Henry Becket to be identified as author of this Work has been asserted by him
in accordance with sections 77 and 78 of the Copyright, Designs and Patents Act 1988

ISBN 978-1-913062-15-6

All rights reserved. No part of this publication may be reproduced, stored in a retrieval
system, copied in any form or by any means, electronic, mechanical, photocopying,
recording or otherwise transmitted without written permission from the author

A CIP catalogue record for this book is available from the British Library

Cover illustration: Tony Husband

Cover and internal design:
sheerdesignandtypesetting.com

Printed and bound by BZGraf S.A.

Contents

Introduction   14

A

Absurd beards   17
Acronyms   17
Agony aunts and astrologers   18
Air conditioning in hotel rooms   19
Aircrew safety demos   19
Airport security   20
Allen keys   21
All French workers   22
Alliteration, tedious and/or contrived   23

All-purpose oriental restaurants   24
All ticket machines   24
Amateur fellow travellers   26
Anaglypta   27
Any TV or radio show with
audience participation   27
Art, modern   28
Atonal music   29
Audience participation   29

B

Back to school   31
Backwards baseball caps   31
Bad tans   31
Bagged salads   33
Bagpipes   33
Bankers   34
Barbeques   34
Beards   35

Bicycle wheels   35
Blatant regifting   37
Boiled eggs   37
Botox   38
Bumbags   39
Business jargon   39
Bus stations   40

C

Cafetières   43
Call centres   43
Cats who refuse expensive cat
food that was their favourite
until you bought in bulk   44
Ceiling light fittings   45

Celebrities   46
Chewing gum packets that disintegrate   46
Christmas commercialities   47
Chuggers   48
Clichés   49
Clingfilm   49

Cocktails	51	Continually-being-reinvented mobile phone chargers	55
Coffee, instant	51	Corporate slogans	55
Combative clothes hangers	51	Cosmetic surgery	56
Concertgoers who start conducting	52	Cruet sets in Indian restaurants	57
Conspiracy theorists	53	Cushions	57
Constant changes to dietary advice	54		
Consultants	54		

D

Daytime TV	59	Drizzle	60
Dim light bulbs	59	Dropped buttered toast	60
Dishwashers	59	Dry January	62
DJs	59	Dumbing down	62
Doormen	59		

E

'Early doors'	65	Estuary English	67
Elastoplast	66	Everyone winning on sports day	68
Email strings	66	Excruciating rustling	68
Energy saving light bulbs	67		

F

F1	71	Flashing images	74
Fake candles	71	Flossing	74
Fanny packs	71	Formula One	75
Fashion	71	French workers	75
Fellow passengers	72	Fruit with meat	76
Film sequels and overexposed TV series	72	Fusion food	76

G

Gatwick Airport	79	'Go large'	80
Generalisations	79	Golf, golfers, golfing clothes, golf clubs	81
Glue that sticks to everything but what you want it to	79	Guessing the wrong platform when arriving at a station	82

H

Hairdressing salon names that
try to be amusing but aren't 85

Half-in/half-out Rawlplugs 85

Hand dryers 86

Hashtags 88

Health & Safety 88

Hen parties 89

High-waisted trousers 90

'Holds knife like pen' (HKLP) 90

Holding patterns (esp. Gatwick
on a Monday morning) 90

Hospitality industry 91

Hospitality suite(s) 91

Hotel room doors 92

Hotel rooms with
incomprehensible light switches 93

Hyper-parenting 94

I

Ice in whisky 97

Inappropriate spending by government,
national, regional and local bodies 97

Inappropriate/out-of-context tat 98

Incompetent cocktail barmen 98

Instant coffee 100

Intrusive noise 101

J

Jet skis 103

K

'Keep calm and...' 105

Kid-centric 105

Kidults 106

L

Lampshades that don't sit right 109

Lazy dog owners 110

Listicles 110

Loo rolls 111

Loo rolls in public conveniences 111

Loud eating 112

Loud keyboard usage 113

Loud mobile phone calls 114

Loud/unamusing ringtones
on mobile phones 114

M

Malls 117

Man flu 117

Merlot 118

Middle managers 118

Midges (and other pointless insects) 120

Ministry of Defence 120

Misplaced apostrophe's 121

Missed opportunities for
amusing 'twinning' 121

Mobile phones 122

Mosquito repellent 122

Motorhomes 124

Movember 125

Musty-smelling hotels 125

N

Name changes 127

Nannying 127

Neck supports on planes 128

New loo rolls with the end
stuck down 129

New Yorkers who loudly announce
themselves and carry on talking
at the tops of their voices 129

No dogs in pubs 130

Noise (offensive) 130

No phone signal 130

No smoking in pubs 132

Not refilling ale glasses but
starting afresh 132

Not washing after weeing, or worse 133

O

Officiousness 137

'On a journey' 138

Onesies 138

Openly displayed bakery products 139

Optics 140

Option to tip offered when
service charge already added 140

Ostentatious physical exercises 141

Out of season food 141

Over-engineering 142

Over-packaging 142

Overtaking on the inside 144

Overused/over-hyped descriptions 144

Oxford Street 144

Oysters that refuse to open 145

P

Pampering 147

Paris 147

Passport control 147

Patronising policemen 149

People who confuse the concepts
of 'working' and 'being at work' 149

People who don't watch where they're
going when they're
looking at their mobile phone 150

People who engage in longwinded

conversations at check-ins 152

People who get into an Underground
carriage before those on board alight 152

People who get to the front of checkout
queue then find to their astonishment
that they have to pay for what they've
put into their trolley 152

People who pretend not to realise
that there is a queue 153

Personnel 154

Pesky pool inflatables 155

Pet shops with appalling names	155	Positive vetting/stereotyping	163
Photocopiers that devour paper and refuse to disgorge it	156	Potholes	163
		PowerPoint	164
Photographs of food outside eating establishments	156	Predictive text	164
		Premature promotions	165
Piercings	157	Pretend working class	166
Piped music	157	Prolonged poppy-wearing	166
Piss-taking cab drivers	158	Pub barmen who are crap at their job	167
		Public displays of affection (PDA)	167
Poetry that isn't	160	Public transport announcements	168
Pointless sports	160	Pubs	170
Policemen	161	Puns	170
Policemen pretending to be helpful	161	Pushy parents	170
Politically correct	162		

Q

Quasi-famous 'lifestyle' bloggers	173	Questionable children's names	174

R

Radio announcers	177	Reply to all	180
Raising the pitch of your voice towards the end of a sentence as if asking a question when you're actually making a statement	177	Restaurants that can't cook as well as I can	181
		Restrooms	181
Rawlplugs	178	Revolving doors that are way more complicated than they need to be	182
Ready meals	178	Ridiculously closely targeted advertising	182
Reality TV	178	Room fresheners	183
Red Nose Day	179	Rubber mats in playgrounds	183
Red ropes outside wannabe in-demand venues	179	Rucksacks	183
		Rules	184
Reloading the dishwasher for no good reason	180	Rustling	185

S

Safe spaces	189	Sales	190
Sagging trousers on youths	189	Sales conferences	190
St Patrick's Day	189	Sarcastic policemen	191

Saturday night TV	192	Sleet	200
Sausages	192	Slush	201
Scented candles	193	Snowflakes	201
Scottish football news	193	So	201
Scrambled eggs	194	Sober for October	202
Screw caps on wine bottles	195	Sourdough bread	203
Selfies	195	South Kensington	203
Sellotape	195	Split infinitives	204
Shouty dads at school sports occasions	197	Sponsorship 'bumpers' at the end of a commercial break	204
Shovel action by people eating	197	Stag weekends	204
Showers that are impossible to work	198	Station stop	205
Simpering	199	Sticky labels that refuse to unstick	205
Sleeping policemen	199	Strategy	206
Sleepy suits	200		

T

Tans	209	The wrong kind of snow/ rain/leaves/sun etc.	217
Taps/plugs that don't work	209	Theme parks	217
Tattoos	210	'There's a good service on all Underground lines'	218
Tautology	211	Things that were once effective but no longer are	218
Team-building	211	Ticket machines	218
Teapots/kettles/jugs that refuse to pour accurately	212	Toilet flushes	219
The easily offended	214	Too frequent firework displays	219
The fashion industry	214	Tourists	220
The M1	214	T-shirts with desperately unfunny slogans	220
The National Anthem	215	Trunki	221
The National Trust	215	Twitter	221
The Proms	216		
The Royal Family	216		

U

Uggs	225	Unnecessary streetlights	228
Unnecessary cushions	225	Unwanted participating in the listening experience of others	228
Unnecessary signs	226	USBs	229

V

Vaping   231

Velour tracksuits   231

Very white trainers   232

VIP areas   232

Virtue-signalling   234

Visitor centres   234

Visual clichés   235

W

Waiting staff who won't catch
your eye   237

W*nkers   238

Warning labels   238

Weather forecasts that contain
nothing of any use   239

'We must do lunch sometime'   240

'We will shortly be landing into…' 240

Wet wipes   241

What the critics say   241

Wheelie luggage that hasn't
mastered the master-slave
relationship   242

'Where's the bathroom?'   243

'Will you do this for me please?'   243

Wine descriptions   243

Wobbly tables in restaurants   244

Woke   245

X

X-rays   247

Y

Young people who can only
communicate by shouting   249

Z

Zeitgeist   251

Acknowledgements   252

About the Author   253

Introduction

Not so long ago, and not for the first time interrupting me whilst I was totally justifiably ranting at the television – MY television, in MY living room, whilst sitting on MY sofa – my wife accused me of being 'so angry, about so many things. ALL the time'.

'You're dead right,' I replied, after a nanosecond's thought. Which set me thinking.

Maybe I wasn't alone? Maybe compiling a compendium of things that could be put right/restored/replaced/repaired/ revisited/re-oriented (and many other relevant things beginning with R, despite my strictures about alliteration, see p.23) would be helpful to others and help rid the world of unrighteous anger. In a nutshell, I could provide a service that might have a chance of preventing us all going to hell in a handcart. And writing as the conservative anarchist which I believe myself to be (the answer the immortal Peter Cook famously gave to a question about his politics, if I recall), this might be a counter to so much that is going wrong in our world.

A list, I thought. That's what it needs – a simple little list of things that make me (and, I suspect, many others) angry. Initially, all I had in mind were a few pages of A4, but in no time at all the list had taken on extraordinary proportions, as you're about to discover. There is just SO MUCH to be angry about. And of course there's nothing wrong with that: logging the relative trivia of what have come to be known as 'First World Problems' is naturally a wonderful form of escapism from what might be perceived as the REAL issues which are making so many people get into such a state.

You would be right in thinking that this process has been cathartic: I've realised that I'm entirely right to be angry, and if this exercise does nothing other than draw attention to the many wrongs that need to be righted – often with little effort required – well, so be it. If, on the other hand, its effects are transformational (as they self-evidently deserve to be), well – what a revolution in human happiness could be contrived. Forget the footling efforts of Cromwell, Galileo, da Vinci, Napoleon, Lenin, Churchill, Newton, and the rest: THIS IS BIG STUFF – not a mere footnote to world history. And I have, of course, only scratched the surface…

A

Absurd beards

Beards that divide into two; straggly beards; beards that conjoin with chest hair; heavy beard growths married with bald heads; a beard worn without a moustache; beards that have clearly not been kempt for decades; beards that play host to alien bodies such as ancient pieces of cheese, vermin or other people's hairs; ginger beards. These are all to be abhorred, for reasons that require no further explanation. As a generalisation, I could also add all those rather poncey hipster beards whose only role presumably is to disguise a weak chin – or add an air of gravitas to someone very clearly lacking it. Oh, and goatees. They even SOUND twee.

The obvious cure is one favoured by stag groups over the ages: get the subject blindingly drunk, then once in a comatose state use clippers/scissors/razor/garden strimmer to remove the offending object(s). Subsequently posting a pair of before/after pictures online should engineer all the aversion therapy 'beardie' will ever need.

Acronyms

These went out with SWALK, NORWICH, OMO etc. (ask your grandparents) sometime during the last century. Yet they are still particularly beloved of marketing people and business consultants, who use them to create the impression that their work is far more complex – and thus high-fee-justifying – than is in fact the case. They are almost always obfuscatory and time-consuming – the opposite of the original attention. TVRs, USP, ROI, BOGOF, BOGADOF, TWATS (no, I made that one up), for example, are all perfectly horrid. More recently, of course, the internet (and particularly social media) has spawned thousands of fatuous new examples like 4YEO, NOYB, FWIW and the ubiquitous and unhelpfully ambiguous LOL. Socially useful examples such as HKLP and NQOCD remain in polite usage, but these should be used sparingly. OTN (of the now), ironically, was OTN a decade or more ago, so anyone saying OTN has clearly been in hibernation for much of this century. Do keep up!

See also Business jargon, HKLP, Middle managers

Agony aunts and astrologers

We all know all agony aunts are writers of fiction, i.e. they create their own fake problems and then concoct an answer. Or are there REALLY so many weirdos in the world with so many weird problems? Sorry, stupid point – OF COURSE there are. But along with newspaper and magazine astrologers, they're little better than funfair fortune tellers of old. Charlatans, the lot of them: I love the story of Kelvin MacKenzie peremptorily firing one 'astrologer' from *The Sun*, his letter beginning, 'As you already know…'

What gives Deirdre/Jane/Suzi/Claire/Marje the chutzpah to think they can counsel poor little Dave from Dagenham about the unsatisfactory size of his willy and what best to do about it? The answer in his case is simple: GET A LIFE! But what you'll get cluttering up your pages is a load of blather about how one day he'll find the right girl…size isn't everything… there are other ways to please her…blah blah…not all women are obsessed with girth or hanker after something hung like the stallion that allegedly pleasured Catherine the Great etc. etc.

And you can bet your bottom dollar that next week's problem on the same page will be a girl whingeing that her boyfriend is 'too big in that department'. To which the obvious answer is not a dozen paragraphs detailing how she could best cope, but rather simply to put Complainant A in direct contact with Complainant B. Job done.

Air conditioning in hotel rooms

How CAN there be 4763 different designs of A/C controls? That really IS capitalism gone mad. And why do they NEVER work in hotel rooms?! That little dial they have, showing fictional temperature values from, say, 15 to 30 degrees – it's just a fantasy to kid you that you're in control – right?! Whatever you do, you soon realise that it's just a dummy control, like those fake burglar alarms, and the dial is connected to nothing more than the plasterboard behind.

And if by some freak of 'hotellery' you come across one that actually has some physical relationship with the air-con machinery, as like as not it will only either dish out a withering blast of Arctic-like air or an unceasing gale of foul-smelling, humid gas like something from the depths of the Patagonian jungles. Take my tip: ask for a hotel room with MANUAL air conditioning, known to previous generations as a 'window', and put up with the traffic noise.

Aircrew safety demos

Actually, this aircraft DOESN'T differ much from others we've flown in…and it's all a load of b★llocks anyway. You know that. We know that. So why should we give it our full attention?

Airport security

How can it be that one week the security people at Gatwick insist that your tablet and laptop MUST be in separate trays, with the tablet removed from its cover, and the next, they brusquely put them both in the same tray, tut-tutting at you as if you're a total idiot, but this time demand that you switch your laptop on.

And why, is it deemed vital for global security one month that you remove your shoes at the same facility, and the next month, when you volunteer to, they look at you as though you're taking the piss so sarcastically that you're in danger of being marched to one side and being subjected to a prolonged anal cavity search by a sadistic brute WITHOUT LATEX GLOVES OR LUBRICATING JELLY?

On the same theme, I am reliably informed that sometimes lipstick qualifies as a liquid, and other times not. How can some airports conceive of cheese as a high explosive, and others not? And can a box of oysters REALLY be mistaken for hand grenades, or a tin of *confit de canard* really be confused with Semtex by some but not all airport security people? If we MUST have absurd rules, please at least apply them consistently.

On this note, you may be interested to know that I was once hauled to one side for an inspection, having walked through the X-ray arch without it sounding an alarm. I then made the schoolboy error of asking why this should be, and was informed in a faux-cockney voice brimming with feigned astonishment at such an absurd question that it was because the man 'had got my number in 'is 'ead.' Anyone sensible would at that point have shrugged and let him have his way, as it were, but this exchange led to a particularly intrusive search involving hands inside trousers. So much so, that I – a glutton for punishment, clearly – made the mistake of querying this as well. 'Do you want to see my inspector?' was the response, and since for once I wasn't in a hurry, I replied that, yes, I would be interested in a gentle chat with the inspector – maybe over a nice cup of lapsang souchong with a thin slice of lemon and a small plate of cucumber sandwiches (well, I didn't actually say that – I'm aware that irony can sometimes be lost on people). The aggressive conversation that ensued climaxed with me being informed that what I had just been subjected to was the 'groin swipe', a new technique specially designed to subdue passengers who evince slight signs of awkwardness. The mind boggles.

See also Gatwick Airport

Allen keys

About a hundred years ago, a no-doubt-somewhat-smug individual from Connecticut – named Allen, unsurprisingly – obtained a patent for a device which has come to torture DIYers ever since. Not because there's anything inherently wrong with the Allen key – just the fact that however carefully you shepherd them, YOU NEVER HAVE THE ONE THAT'S THE RIGHT SIZE. Some well-intentioned relative probably gave you a neat little bunch one Christmas back in the day that all hung together in a cluster, but whenever you go back to them to tighten something that's worked loose, the only one that fits has inexplicably gone missing. Why do there have to be so many variations of hexagon dimension for Chrissake? Is there any more need for this degree of variety than smartphone manufacturers continually reinventing the charging socket so that you end up with a tangled drawerful of redundant near-identical but fatally different plugs?

And then, to compound your irritation, every so often you come across the version that's SQUARE not hexagonal. What's that all about? I mean – you'd have to be thoroughly OCD to keep a set of square Allen-type keys to hand in case they might come in handy? And even if you did, you can bet anything you like that the exact size you want will be nowhere to be found.

Mind you, isn't that true of ALL DIY? I cannot be alone in NEVER having exactly the right thing to hand for whatever I need to do: I have jars and tins containing thousands of assorted screws and bolts accumulated over the decades, but it's a safe bet that I'll be off to the ironmonger for a packet of two dozen new ones (when I only need one) because NONE of them is right.

See also Continually-being-reinvented mobile phone chargers

All French workers

It will probably come as no surprise to you that the French are so work-shy that there is a website specifically dedicated to listing current and upcoming strikes. cestlagreve.fr lists dozens of industrial actions, as the unintentionally ironic euphemism has it, every day of the year, every year.

But supposing you CAN find a French worker to do your bidding, you can be pretty sure it will go wrong on you. Thirty-plus years of suffering at the hands of French gardeners, roofers, pool-men, plumbers, glaziers, electricians, *maçons generales*, tree surgeons, plasterers, mechanics, boat repairers, painters, carpenters, aerial-installers, tilers, kitchen-fitters, heating specialists and more attest to the essential truth of this sweeping generalisation. Sometimes they smile when they f*ck you up; sometimes they're morose; and sometimes the non-delivery is delivered with a Gallic shrug – just as in cod movies from the fifties.

Whatever, the fun of it depicted in *A Year in Provence* all those years ago belongs to a fictitious golden age. Even if they start off promisingly, the French worker will inevitably rapidly go off, like a ripe reblochon left exposed on a humid day, when most of it simply runs off the plate while your back is turned and you're left to contemplate a small, repellent, rubbery residue. My simple advice? DON'T GO THERE (as the current voguish saying has it). One of the best things we ever did was to import our very own Pole from Kensington to do some painting in return for a holiday. It was a life-reaffirming experience for us, and the locals are still talking years after the event about the miracles that were achieved in the space of a few days.

Alliteration, tedious and/or contrived

All junior speechwriters, second-rate copywriters and third-rate politicians adore the alliterative device. This, they are convinced, makes for a decidedly dexterous demonstration of their literary adroitness. No, it doesn't (see previous sentence). It's easy to do, overused and a poor substitute for original writing: most people grow out of it in about Year 8. Those that don't…well, they just damn well – determinedly, deliberately – don't.

See also Misplaced apostrophe's, Split infinitives

All-purpose oriental restaurants

Chinese – good. Thai – good. Vietnamese – good. Etc., etc. But ALL of them at the same restaurant? I don't think so – the end result will be a bland, slightly spicy, vaguely Far-Eastern-style meal with very little appetite-appeal. A dead giveaway will be the name – invariably something generically offensive like Fuk U or the one three doors further down the street called Fuku 2. Another will be the pictures of the food, where with a disarming sense of honesty every dish will look almost exactly the same, off-brown with a hint of beige. Another useful rule of thumb is, the larger and more grotesque the Lucky Cat doing its cod-Nazi salute in the window, the more likely you are to have a thoroughly dismal experience. Walk on by (there's probably a half-decent kebab shop two minutes away).

All ticket machines

Has ANYONE EVER come across a ticket machine that is intuitively straightforward to use? It doesn't matter what station you're at, which country you're in, what language is required, the chances are that the machine you're trying to use has been intentionally, ingeniously designed so as to thwart your best intentions, with the likely result that you'll end up travelling without a ticket – assuming you can surmount the barrier – thereby depriving the operating company of income. Oh – hang on, I've just realised it's a deliberate business strategy: no ticket means the operating company doesn't just get the price of issuing a ticket when you get caught but the added bonus of the grotesquely large fine it will exact for discovering that

ORIENTAL
RESTAURANT

CHINA   NORTH
         KOREA   THAILAND

Bread
and
water

you haven't purchased a valid ticket for travel and so are in contravention of the rules of carriage.

See also Officiousness

Amateur fellow travellers

It must be getting on for half a century now that flying with any liquids of more than 100 ml by volume has been outlawed, so – no, lady who's standing in front of me in the queue, please don't waste my time trying to negotiate acceptance of half a dozen bottles of Lambrini for the flight and a gallon of cheap scent for your fortnight on the Costa del Sol. And while you're at it, best get your other half to take his clunking metal-clad biker boots off now, before he is instructed to do so and then discovers that it is a full half-hour process to dismantle the assembly.

Oh, and now you've found out belatedly that you've got a brace of iPads and a machete in your carry-on. How did those get there?! Silly old you – maybe you could lend me the machete and I'll make good use of it.

These are the same people who, when they get onto the plane in front of you, spend an inordinate length of time standing in the gangway, discussing what items of clothing to discard and what they will require from their various bags by way of in-flight entertainment. For all of one and a half hours, which you already know they will spend comatose, or worse, audibly loving each other up.

And then, on landing, they'll be first up before the 'fasten your seat belts sign' has been switched off, and trying to barge their way past you in defiance of all conventions, before they realise they've forgotten a bag/weapon/child and barge back past you again, as like or not with a nausea-inducing whiff of that vile perfume they've drenched themselves in rather than let it go to waste at the X-ray machine.

Anaglypta

Anyone who went to university in the last few decades or sent offspring there is certain to share my loathing of Anaglypta, and more specifically the way it tears apart when you so much as glance at it. This always leads to the other kind of tears when you come to hand the room back at the end of the year, and it's obvious that your hurried application of Tipp-Ex/white felt-tip/chewing gum isn't going to prevent the landlord from docking the entire rent deposit for repairs.

Anaglypta can also cause injuries, as anyone who has ever overnighted in a cheap hotel will attest: just make sure you never rub a tender part of your anatomy on the wall next to your bed. You have been warned!

Any TV or radio show with audience participation

Question Time…Any Questions…Any Answers… in fact pretty much any programme featuring the voices of 'ordinary people' (and by the way, am I alone in detesting that phrase?!). Who in their right mind wants to listen to the semi-formed thoughts of a lot of self-promoters being voiced in the supposed safety of one's own living room? I for one definitely do not. Why not replace such horrors with half-an-hour's transmission of a log-fire burning or an aquarium? These are readily available for a relatively small sum and are sure to be much more informative and less likely to cause anguish.

See also Reality TV

Art, modern

One of the truest exchanges ever written in any book, in any language, in any era, was in *Brideshead Revisited*, when Charles Ryder is asked by Cordelia, 'Modern art is all bosh, isn't it?' Thankfully, without hesitation, the answer comes, 'Oh yes – great bosh'. 'Nuff said. That brief, prescient answer, given with a languid delivery that brooked no dissent, unquestionably made Jeremy Irons' career – and quite possibly Evelyn Waugh's before him.

And was there EVER a more obvious example of the emperor's new clothes syndrome? You stand in front of a scribble that might have been drawn by a toddler, and are expected to see all sorts of meaningful stuff. You don't, naturally. Then someone tells you it's worth $50m, and your mind starts to wander: 'If I owned that piece of crap, I could sell it, and buy lots of really good stuff – maybe even a PROPER painting!' Please don't tell me I'm the only person who has ever experienced that thought process, standing, less than transfixed, in front of a hideous example of modern art that betrays no artistic talent whatsoever. Give me a landscape… a pulchritudinous nude…flying ducks, even. But please confine your Rothkos, Kandinskys, Pollocks (not sure about the spelling of this) and the rest to the restricted-access storage areas where they'll cause least offence.

See also Atonal music

Atonal music

That bloody Arnold Schoenberg has perhaps got even more to answer for than the wretches who invented the Arndale Centre. Classical music was tootling along, perfectly inoffensively, minding its own tuneful business, when along comes 1921 and his ghastly *Suite für Klavier* (NOT an English composition, note). I mean, whoever writes music to sound intentionally not just discordant – but physically painful? Well, a lot of people, so it turns out. Even more weirdly, some people learn to play it, and others pay to listen to it. Astonishing.

Audience participation

See Any TV or radio show with audience participation, Reality TV

B

Back to school

A retail/online promotion that invariably commences at the very start of the longest holiday of the school year, thus inducing palpitations in school attendees of a nervous disposition and a sense of joy/doom amongst those parents who for the first time in a year have to cope with the continuous presence of their offspring. To make the experience even less life-affirming, the words are almost always printed in a childlike font, gaily coloured, with at least one of the letters written backwards and sometimes unintentionally enhanced by the device of spelling school as SKOOL. Does NO ONE appreciate the irony of this?

See also Premature promotions

Backwards baseball caps

No one has ever been able to explain to me why a baseball cap – if it has to be worn at all – should be worn backwards. It is surprising that no one has invented a cap with the peak sewn onto the reverse, but maybe that's just too obvious. It is perfectly understandable that those chaps in the Eighth Army in North Africa chose to wear those hats with the bit of cloth protecting the back of your neck from the noonday sun, but is it really necessary at the Emirates Stadium on a damp December evening?

Bad tans

It really doesn't need me to say it, but surely the worst imaginable tan (aside from the lobster-pink super-peely variety boasted by Scotsmen who spend fifty weeks of the year in driving rain on some godforsaken moor chasing capercaillie and the remaining fortnight baking on a vile beach in Famagusta) is that achieved by girls who haven't mastered the strange business of fake tanning. They're the ones you see queuing outside a nightclub with streaky orange legs looking for all the world like an amateur watercolourist's rendering of a winter sunset. The only bit of them that will have a uniform ochre hue will be their knuckles and their knees and the bits between their fingers, where they've either not realised how much colouring has accumulated or they've failed to wash after applying. Yuk.

But even with a naturally acquired tan, why is THAT invariably so patchy? Why is one's back brown and stomach white, and, conversely, why are the backs of legs white and thighs brown? And are the insides of everyone's arms totally resistant to the effects of ultraviolet? The trouble is that the remedies to these common problems are – let's face it – borderline weird. John Mortimer captured something of this in *Summer's Lease* – the obsessive labours of the determinedly tanning – but I've seen some memorably eccentric behaviour. At the mild end of the spectrum are the people with their arms splayed out, crucifix-like, to tan the underside of the arms. Have you ever tried this position, and realised how damned uncomfortable it is to hold for more than a few moments? Puts me in mind of Lucian Freud's nude posers, who typically had to visit an osteopath for months after a prolonged sitting. Then there was the oiled-up German couple on the beach in Huelva, both glistening from head to toe, who had an old-school alarm clock with them which alarm reminded them to turn every fifteen minutes, as if they were a couple of pork chops. Best of all, though, was the entirely naked, well-lubed Dutch guy we once witnessed, who every few minutes would delicately pick up his organ at the business end between forefinger and thumb and neatly lay it out across his thigh the other side down. That clearly takes OCD behaviour to an entirely new – if oddly admirable – level: we just hoped his partner would later appreciate the lengths to which he had gone to in order to attain peak perfection. Ho ho.

Bagged salads

A bizarre fetish of the modern age, and another giving credence to Becket's First Law of Fatuity: if there's no need for a product, please don't hasten the demise of our planet by bringing it to market. As far as I can ascertain, these are essentially just confettis of nitrogen, carbon dioxide and not-so-dilute-that-you-can't-smell-or-taste-it chlorine, with a few scraps of greenish leaves (often yellow, as it happens) thrown in to kid you that you're buying something remotely tasty and healthy.

Why not just buy a good old Webbs lettuce in season, or an iceberg if you must, or even a little gem – or grow your own. Even a self-respecting rabbit should turn its nose up at a cellophane sack of out-of-season wilting leaves of dubious origin with a size forty-seven carbon footprint. I blame the British Leafy Salads Association (there really is one) 'cos you have to blame someone…

Bagpipes

An abomination, unless your morale needs lifting as you clamber up one of the Normandy beaches under withering machine-gun fire on D-Day. Otherwise, they serve no useful purpose whatsoever. Obviously. If you're born south of Hadrian's Wall you'll know what I mean. Whoever first gave the description of a gentleman as 'someone who knows how to play the bagpipes, but doesn't' is clearly genius.

Bankers

Cockney rhyming slang for w*nkers. Orig. unknown. Pointless description for a category of worker that has no tangible connection with what the rest of the world understand by banking whatsoever, and are only here to f*ck us all up.

Barbeques

Look, I like a sausage or a burger as much as the next man, but MUST it have the consistency of tar-coated gravel on the outside and be absolutely raw within and probably rife with E. coli? Oh, and cold, to boot. Why, pray, is it that all the normal rules of what constitute pleasurable eating are so often suspended just because you're having supper *al fresco*? Do we HAVE to pretend that it's SUCH FUN, as after the first ill-advised bite we have no choice but to discreetly chuck a raw, charred piece of what was advertised as chicken into the shrubbery, and end up merely with a miserable plate of wilting lettuce as a substitute for dinner? Oh, and some vile warm rosé from the local offy.

And then, at the other extreme, when someone rightly decides that the basic fare of bangers, burgers and bits of chicken just will not do, why do they have to go the whole hog and inflict an arty neo-Blumenthal mess of something unidentifiable on their fellow diners? In your heart of hearts you know no one's going to like it, much as they might pretend to love your creative deployment of unlikely ingredients, almost certainly flagged up as a fusion of something or other from two wildly differing and thoroughly inappropriate cooking cultures.

It's a barbeque, dammit, not a competition – why not just give us a decent shoulder of lamb or an honest *côte de boeuf*? Proper food, easily sorted, and not pretending to be anything it's not. And really, there's no excuse for either to be anything other than lightly charred on the outside and healthily pink inside: it's perfectly possible to swig your succession of Peronis with one hand whilst adjusting/turning/setting the meat to rest etc. with the other. This is the voice of experience speaking.

Beards

See Absurd beards

Bicycle wheels

If you've ever been a cyclist you'll know exactly where this is going. To pump up a tyre in a way that is ergonomically efficient – comfortably, even – you really want the little valve on the wheel to be somewhere near the five or seven o'clock position on the wheel. Nearer the top of the wheel, you'll be contorting yourself and the connector to your pump in such a way that you'll probably injure yourself and damage valve, pump, or both. So how is it, then, that when you come to lean your bike against the wall, the valve on not just one but BOTH wheels is in exactly the opposite position to what you want? Every time. I had my first bike at primary school and am now the cycling recipient of an old-age pension, and having had four children's bikes in two countries to sort out over the years, as well as my own, you may correctly imagine that I have a huge store of empirical evidence on which to base this finding.

Blatant regifting

If someone makes a present of a delicately scented candle overpackaged in a jar in some tissue paper and a box, it's a fair bet that they are regifting. I mean, they can't REALLY think that you're the prime target audience for a bit of tat like that, can they – especially if you're a bloke the wrong side of fifty? The only even more blatant and unforgiveable form of regifting is when they give something to you THAT YOU'D GIVEN TO THEM EIGHT MONTHS EARLIER. There is only one set of additional circumstances that makes this behaviour acceptable – enjoyable, even – and that is when you yourself were passing on something which had been given to you inappropriately some time before. Other halves are known to maintain significant stocks of unwanted gifts of this type, which helps form a sizeable chunk of the black economy, being a basic form of barter. It is entirely likely that the UK's productivity/consumption figures are wildly understated entirely because of this, making a compelling argument for including a generous estimate in this regard that would thereby help propel us almost to the top of the world rankings.

Boiled eggs

Why oh why does the world find it so difficult to boil an egg in such a way that the would-be breakfaster has at least a percentage chance of finding it appetising? It should NEVER be solid. It should NEVER be runny, which is worse. It should NEVER be glutinous, with sick-making see-through bits that seem to stick to everything. Oh, and it should never be fertilised. As any fule kno, the white should be absolutely firm (like a proper panna cotta) and the yolk should be a warm golden-yellow and just runny enough to be able to dip a few soldiers in for a period of perhaps three or four minutes. A small heap of freshly ground salt and pepper should naturally be to hand, for the purposes of dipping.

It's not nuclear physics, though one might think so. Look, just take an egg that's no more than a few days old. Boil some water. When it's boiling, lower your egg gently in with the aid of an appropriate-sized spoon. Give it, say, four and a bit minutes, then gently lift it out. If it dries quickly in the spoon, the chances are that it's perfect. Place it in an egg cup, carefully slice the top off, and hey presto – a perfect boiled-egg experience awaits. Divorce petitions have been served for lesser offences than confronting one's other half with an inexpertly cooked boiled egg, so it's best to get it right.

See also Scrambled eggs

Botox

Why anyone would want willingly to have bacteria injected into, for example, their face defeats me. Especially when it may even cause vile side effects, coming from the same family that causes botulism. But putting that to one side, why anyone would WANT the Botox smile-deadening effect in the first place I find utterly incomprehensible. The little lines that come from a life well-lived convey so much personality, whereas those 'celebs' whose every fatuous activity is absurdly over-documented have all the potential for genuine facial expressions of a piece of cheap hardboard – and almost certainly with less of interest to communicate.

And now I read that in the States vacuous chaps are opting for Brotox, administered in blokey mancave-style clinics, where the walls are adorned with framed sweaty football shirts and stuffed moose heads. We really are heading to hell in a handcart, but in this era our companions in the tumbril will be hordes of waxy, dead-faced thirty-somethings a bit like the extras in *The Stepford Wives*, almost certainly with voices like them, too. Hell might actually be preferable to the journey there…

See also Cosmetic surgery, Reality TV

Bumbags

Here's a useful clue as to why sporting one of these items is not a good idea: the name. You will LOOK like – and considered as – a bum – the more so if you suspend this hideous item under your gut for all the world like a kangaroo pouch transplant.

Of course, if you're from the other side of the pond, you will proclaim that this is a 'fanny pack'. For guidance on the desirability or otherwise of strapping one of these to your midriff, see para 1 above.

See also Backwards baseball caps

Business jargon

It's just office work, guys, not nuclear science: GET OVER IT! Do not blue-sky it, take it offline, get the team on board with it, or run it up the flagpole to see who salutes. Nobody wants to know! So please stop holding a mirror up to your customers, circling back, and the like, and take your Boston matrices, cash cows, ballparks, J-I-Ts, and all the rest of the nonsense and stick it where the sun don't shine. WTC, JFDI by close-of-play and stop wittering on about it.

See also Acronyms, Middle managers

Bus stations

There is something vaguely pleasing about a bus, but equally there is something faintly sinister about a bus station. Is it the sense that after hours, buses go there to breed? Or more prosaically, is it more about the people who typically loiter there? Whatever – best avoided (especially after dark, for reasons that should be self-evident, especially if you're someone with delicate sensibilities and worry about what a sump or a flange might actually look like in the flesh, so to speak).

C

Cafetières

Hideous contraptions, especially the bigger versions, capable not just of producing substandard coffee, but spraying jets of boiling hot brown liquid in all directions. That strange springy plunger ring is always either too big or too small: too small and all the grounds get squirted back into the coffee with the force of Old Faithful, swirling around to produce an undrinkable sludge; too big and the whole glass container will shatter, necessitating a visit to A&E with all the attendant horrors that implies, such as the strong likelihood of contracting MRSA.

Call centres

The only good thing about call centres is that they are NEVER based in Birmingham or the environs. Funny that (no suggestions on a postcard, please. No, really – PLEASE). Beyond that, they are of course all utterly hateful. And hopeless. 'For anything else, press Option Four.' NO! I don't want to listen to your gruesome sub-techno music a nanosecond longer. There MUST be a real person, lurking somewhere in your building, who is capable of a timely, comprehensible, rational response to an intelligent question. In the language that I speak, even if you're not working in the same country as I'm calling from. No. Silly me. I must cast off my cynical carapace and embrace the brave new world of the semi-automated, semi-literate 'customer-facing' cadre – which means facing up to the fact that millions of acres of commercial buildings the world over are stuffed to the gills with people who are highly trained to f*ck you up in every way imaginable.

Because you might be – or be trying to be – a customer. Or trying to stop being one: now THERE'S a challenge (yes, I'm talking about YOU Sky, and you BT…).

Oh, and of course the next thing that will happen after a thoroughly dispiriting forty-five minute experience is that they will send out a twenty-four page automated questionnaire to your mobile phone inviting you to rate the quality of the service you have just endured in absurd detail: 'please take a few moments to describe what was particularly positive'. Yeah, right – now that's about as likely to happen as me accepting that they really do mean 'your call is important to us'.

Cats who refuse expensive cat food that was their favourite until you bought in bulk

On the one hand I rather approve of the independence and bloody-mindedness of the typical domestic cat. But on the other, when it comes to rejecting what they have been insisting for weeks beforehand was their all-time favourite food, this bloody-mindedness can verge on the callous. It's a wind-up, isn't it? They saw the Ocado man dropping off half a ton of it and thought:

'Hey, this'll be a laugh, I'll pretend to have gone off it just to see the look on their faces and hear the intemperate things they'll go on to say. Then an hour or so later I'll do that leg-rubbing, tail-curling, purring thing and they'll adore me even more, recognising my unpredictability for the thoroughly desirable quality it clearly is. I mean, if they want tiresome, bland consistency in a pet, they can always swap me for a spaniel.'

Ceiling light fittings

If, like me, you've had occasion to install a ceiling light fitting yourself, you'll know exactly what this rant-ette is all about. On the one hand, you'll want some decent space in which to manoeuvre your fingers, screwdriver, pliers and suchlike. On the other, the aesthetic requirements of the device demand that such space be so limited as to make the task all but unachievable. That, plus the fact that your face is twisted at an absurd angle uncomfortably close to the ceiling, with you teetering on a stepladder and your varifocals rendering you all but blind as you attempt to focus on that wretched little plastic block in which you have to stick a series of tiny wires.

But then – you've done it: you've successfully screwed the 'base' of the fitting into the ceiling without bringing half the plaster down; you've poked all the wires into their impossibly small apertures; you've tightened all the tiny screws you can see; you've tucked the ever-resentful little plastic block out of harm's way; you've tested that the light actually worked; you've positioned the fitting over its 'mothership' on the ceiling and screwed it tight. Back down the stepladder, flick the switch and…nothing. Not even an encouraging flicker.

You knew that was going to happen, didn't you? With a grim inevitability, as you tightened the things that fasten the bits of the light fitting together, one of those rebellious little wires inside has worked its way loose – Christ alone knows which one, or why. But it always does.

My advice at this point is to do nothing other than – hands trembling – pour yourself a morale-boosting, consciousness-blurring, blood-pressure-ameliorating whisky (no ice, see p.97). Definitely do nothing more until the next day. Or ever. It's probably better to move house altogether and forever hold forth on the aesthetic demerits of central lights altogether and how occasional lamps are SO much more satisfactory, ambience-wise.

Celebrities

Over-exposed nonentities, by and large. So…oxymoronic. Or mostly just moronic.

Chewing gum packets that disintegrate

You open one of Mr Wrigley's small tubes of chewing gum tablets, pop one in your mouth, and the packet goes back into your jacket pocket. Within minutes the entire contents have been disgorged unawares, and when you next put your hand in there, they've all congealed into a vile sticky mess that no dry cleaner will ever be able to dislodge. That lump is there for good. And what about 'Hollywood' gum in that natty little box with the fliptop lid with the aperture in it: has anyone EVER been able to get a piece out? They only seem to emerge *en masse* when left to their own devices, rather like lemmings, in the dark crevices of your briefcase, and never when you actually want one.

But what IS it with packaging that isn't fit for purpose? I recall once being presented with a designer's portfolio which featured the container for Eucryl tooth powder as an example of his talent, and all I could think of was that every time I opened its oh-so-clever lid some of the contents spilled out. I reckon half the volume went this way.

And it's not just packaging. Why do Apple make it so fiendishly difficult to open an iPad to replace the SIM? Why are modern-day car bonnets near impossible to open? And why are waiters' knives so useless at opening a bottle of wine?

See also Over-packaging

Christmas commercialities

Pointless. What proportion of annual GDP do you suppose is frittered away on the purchase of the vast quantities of fancy crepe paper, foil, cardboard and the like which go to make up the typical Christmas cracker? And as for the junk inevitably discovered therein – the wretched paper hat, dire joke (or – recent horror of horrors – 'conversation starter'), and surprise 'gift' (who actually ENJOYS unsolvable metal puzzles, or the excitement of a miniature padlock with a key that doesn't work?)…

I always assume that there is a small freelance army of retired advertising copywriters who eke out their retirement from the groan-inducing scribbles that fall out of our crackers on Christmas Day. Can SOMEONE find out who they are and put them out of their – and our – misery, before they graduate to devising bad puns for pet shops, tattoo parlours and the like?

And as for Christmas jumpers – amusing the first year that they were popular (mid-seventeenth century?) but no longer. Especially as they are now apparently compulsory in many places of business at least one day a year. The more LED lights they contain, the more likely they are to be ghastly, obvs.

Which naturally brings me to Christmas movies. Why are they always set in New England? How come it's always just the perfect amount of snow?! Why is almost the entire cast so GODDAM SOPPY? Do they only have 100 per cent perfectly formed Christmas trees? Why is the music track always so banal? Why are they never all pissed? And why does the vile mother-in-law always eventually come good, when you know that in real life she'll throw an epi and spend most of Christmas Day in a sulk in the spare room, leaving everyone else downstairs debating how long to leave her before they weaken and encourage her back down.

I suppose, to be fair, the Americans gave us the antidote to all this in *National Lampoon's Christmas Vacation*, but even that too often veers dangerously towards drippy territory. As an indicator of the huge volume of films in this *oeuvre*, there is now a non-stop Christmas TV Channel up and running for a month during Advent. John Logie Baird surely cannot have had this in mind all those years ago when he was working on what became the television set – and if he did, well, no posthumous punishment is too severe for him.

Chuggers

Please, go away, and take your piercings, tattoos, name badge and clipboard with you! If we want to contribute to charity, there are easier ways than being stopped in the street for a half-hearted conversation with an ill-informed, commission-incentivised quasi do-gooder. Better to go and work for *Médecins sans Frontières* or some such, rather than pester people going about their everyday business. And have you ever tried to deflect the inevitable eyes-filled-with-scorn-boring-into-your-back-how-could-you-be-such-a-mean-bastard reaction when you decline to add to their score sheet? I have, and wished I hadn't, the rationale that maybe you'd rather donate direct to a charity where you KNOW it's not all going to be frittered on business-class flights, fatuous week-long conferences in the Maldives and expensive advertising campaigns (oh – and your chugger's commission) isn't one that resonates well with your average well-intentioned street hawker, or so I've found. It's easier, on balance, just to let them assume that you really ARE a mean-spirited bastard without a generous bone in your body and no fellow-feeling whatsoever for the travails of much of the human race, and let them bathe in a glow of monumental self-satisfaction – BECAUSE THEY'RE NOT LIKE YOU. Trust me, when they grow up, they will be.

Clichés

As the well-worn cliché has it, almost always a substitute for lazy thinking. 'And metmen say there's more to come!' is one of the classic examples. 'And finally…' is another one. Football-speak is of course full of them ('the lads left nothing out there'). So is advertising, as you would expect, and public relations handouts, and *The Sun*'s front and back pages. 'SPRING INTO SUMMER!' – that's a typical headline. 'SOFA SO GOOD' another that no downmarket furnishing store can ever resist using to promote a particularly hideous three-piece suite. Weather forecasters regale us with talk of 'spits and spots' and tell us the weather's going to be 'misty and murky'. And the NHS is always 'world class' or 'the envy of the world' – and the beliefs of people are always 'firmly held'. On a lighter note, I for one am delighted to find that cleavages and charms are invariably 'ample', but ARE they always?

Clingfilm

Never was a descriptor – in the case 'cling' – more aptly coined. It just won't stop clinging to itself. You can ignore that serrated

edge on the packaging: that will never work, naturally. So you resort to unpicking it by hand to find the free edge. That's all well and good at the start of the roll – but when it's halfway through? By then it has become a mass of solid plastic, with annoying bumps and ridges theoretically showing you where to start. But no – that's just grown there over a period of weeks to mislead. What I really want to know is – why does clingfilm cling to itself immovably when it's on the spool that it arrives in, BUT NEVER AGAIN when you really want it to? Another of modern life's profound mysteries, incapable of resolution.

Cocktails

See Incompetent cocktail barmen

Coffee, instant

See Instant coffee

Combative clothes hangers

How can it be, that clothes hangers – which, after all, are just supposed to hang about, waiting for gainful employment – have an ability to interfere in the normal running of everyday life in a way never conceived of by their inventors, an achievement variously attributed to President Thomas Jefferson and an otherwise anonymous denizen of Connecticut?

Whether they're made of metal, plastic or wood, or a combination of these materials; whether they're purchased or stolen; whether they are long in the tooth or fresh from the dry-cleaners – they display an inability to coexist peaceably with each other in a way which is reminiscent of the Great Powers in the run-up to World War I. They are forever getting in a tangle, no matter how hard you try to apply a modicum of order in your wardrobe or provide reasonable space for them to live in harmony with each other. There is a concept in the history of empire-building known as the contiguous area theory, which holds that nations ineluctably expand into the neighbouring neck of the woods, whether free space is available or not. I have come to the conclusion that this concept equally applies to the wardrobe, with almost equally fraught outcomes in which you are left with a cat's cradle of coat hangers, never again to be disentangled without the threat of serious violence to the participants, and with a similar likelihood of it all ending in tears.

Concertgoers who start conducting

Look matey, you may THINK you have all the makings of being the next Von Karajan, but kindly restrain yourself when you're in a concert audience. No one else wants to know that you can work out whether the piece is in 4:4 or 3:4 time. If you must 'conductalong' please do so in the privacy of your own home or automobile, where the risk of distracting fellow listeners is minimal. Tapping on your knee or continuously moving your legs to the beat is equally infra dig, obviously.

See also The Proms

Conspiracy theorists

The CIA did NOT fly two passenger jets into the WTC for the hell of it. A B-52 bomber HASN'T been found on the moon. Roswell is merely a collection of sheds on an airfield in a remote part of the States. The BBC isn't intentionally trying to create a nation of dumbwits. GET REAL, guys! Stuff happens, for which the best explanation is normally a series of unhappy accidents/coincidences conjoining to make a noticeable circumstance. You can't blame the Americans/Jews/Arabs/Muslims/Christian fundamentalists/vegans/carnivores/*Daily Mail*/BBC for every woe.

The trouble is, the views of the relatively well-adjusted majority are continually undermined by the extreme contrariness of real-life events, so making the opinions of conspiracy theorists more likely to become a widely believed statement of the bleedin' obvious. Donald Trump became President of the US. Around the same time a woman who did colouring-in at Oxford became Prime Minister and a non-retired third-rate student activist became Leader of the Opposition. A train on the LNER arrived on time at its destination. It didn't rain on August Bank Holiday. The solution is simple: question EVERYTHING and EVERYBODY – apart from immigration staff at airports in the States, who have had their sense of humour surgically removed and are inclined to have you banged up for months in a top-security correctional facility for daring to wonder why something was being done in a particularly weird way.

Constant changes to dietary advice

Carbs good, carbs bad. Meat good, meat bad. Veg good, veg bad. Fat…sugar…fruit…juice…butter…red wine…coffee – in the past couple of decades there can hardly be a food/drink type that hasn't been successively praised as the holy grail of healthy eating, then comprehensively dissed months later as near-lethal in the next fatuous bit of dodgy research that does the rounds. But there's nothing new under the sun: apparently, cornflakes were originally devised not least as a means of inhibiting excessive masturbation. But I suppose anything that kept both hands busy would have worked. Here's my advice: avoid breakfast cereals obviously, and do what Evelyn Waugh chose to do when his doctor advised eating more fruit: add an extra slice of lime/lemon to your G&T.

Consultants

Acceptable in a hospital, but nowhere else. Armies of consultants have been known to descend on dying companies with the effect of hastening their demise through syphoning off vast sums of money. In most instances these days, the word consultant in the context of business is simply a pretentious term for freelancer. Or otherwise unemployed. The extreme irony is that we all know of people who've been made expensively redundant on a Friday from central or local government, or an overweight commercial organisation, or the armed forces, then immediately rehired after the weekend as a consultant on a pay scale hugely in excess of the salary they just gave up. Has ANYONE ever understood why? There's probably even a consultancy sector that specialises in exactly this process…

And while I'm on about the weird world of business, can we please ban the word 'executive', as in a descriptor of middle-management, with their attendant 'executive suites' at gruesome corporate hospitality events, 'executive rooms' in hotels, 'executive homes', blah blah blah. There was once even a 'Jaguar executive' for pity's sake! Imagine paying out something like forty grand only to end up driving around with that phrase stamped on your rear end for everyone to snigger at.

See also Middle managers

Continually-being-reinvented mobile phone chargers

Who hasn't got a drawer…a cupboard…a roomful, even, of assorted mobile phone chargers going back to the eighties? Black ones, white ones, cream ones, grey ones, fat ones, thin ones, long ones, short ones, frayed ones; ones with embarrassingly minute 'male' ends; ones with impressive ends; ones with an array of adaptors attached; others that have long since lost their adaptor.

And none of them likely to be of any use to anyone ever again. Producers have made squillions from continually reinventing these, clearly totally unnecessarily, and the only answer is to throw away any adaptor the moment you stop using that phone. Otherwise, you are likely to lose all sense of reason.

Corporate slogans

OK, OK, I'll just do it! But do I really have to wear an exorbitantly expensive pair of cleverly branded but otherwise very ordinary trainers at the same time? I'll just get on and do it in my own way, if it's all the same to you, ideally in a battered pair of deck shoes. I wish it sounded less of an instruction and more of a suggestion: as such I'm very strongly inclined to go out and buy a sensible pair of brogues, just to be difficult. Take that Mr Kappa, or whatever your name is.

JFDI: now THAT's more like it. And funny in a way that FCUK manifestly was not. I cannot help pronouncing the phrase in full in the exasperated tone employed back in the day by my father when I came up with yet another excuse for not starting my homework.

And while we're on the subject of fatuous brand slogans, don't you hate all those corporate phrases typically seen on the side of lorries, employing what are technically known as 'verbals': 'delivering value', 'making the world a better place', 'putting the customer first', blah blah blah. Oh for the good old days when brand statements were an unequivocal statement of the bleeding obvious: 'McVitie's Bake a Better Biscuit'; 'Irn Bru: made in Scotland from Girders'; and my personal favourite – stuck on the side of a derelict factory, and enjoyed on a daily basis for years on my way to work – 'Lesme have a way with the cocoa bean'. (Note to corporate strategists – ensure that your strapline can stand the test of time: Lesme's way with the cocoa bean – whatever it was – clearly WASN'T so effective after all. The clue is in the phrase 'derelict factory'.)

See also T-shirts with desperately unfunny slogans

Cosmetic surgery

If you were a badly disfigured Battle of Britain pilot there is every reason to be thankful for cosmetic surgery, and you are to be hugely admired for the sacrifice you have made and the bravery in putting up with the pain. And there are other completely understandable reasons for cosmetic surgery with which one can but sympathise.

But equally, there are millions of instances where it is more than regrettable – it is just bizarre. And these are normally the ones where elective surgery (i.e. you have actively chosen to have it done) has taken place, maybe to get a stint on *Love Island*, with a tidier underneath, fake boobs or an artificially enhanced six-pack. One thinks of such unfortunates as the Bride of Wildenstein or the wretched Jordan and wonders – for God's sake…WHY? Look, it didn't do Frankenstein much good in the end, did it…so best ignore those strange ads for surgeons in the Turkish hinterland that promise a bigger bum, chin, willy etc. etc. and remember the old adage: it's not what you've got, it's what you do with it.

See also Botox

Cruet sets in Indian restaurants

First, all tables in all curry houses are too small for the selection of dishes which will inevitably crowd them once your order arrives. And second, all dishes in all curry houses are relatively spicy. So please tell me why they all have that nasty little stainless steel cruet set, with its damp salt and powdery white pepper whose manufacture as any fule kno involves the use of pee? One of life's eternal mysteries.

Cushions

See Unnecessary cushions

D

Daytime TV

It should be obvious that the daytime is for being out and about – not for slumping in front of the TV. Come the revolution, any broadcaster attempting to air programmes between the hours of, say, 10 a.m. and 4 p.m. will be sentenced to five years solitary, with only a TV for company, endlessly playing a looped tape of the most cringeworthy TV padding ever devised.

See also Simpering

Dim light bulbs

See Energy-saving light bulbs

Dishwashers

See Reloading the dishwasher for no good reason

DJs

See Radio announcers, Simpering

Doormen

Ridiculous. In their stupid hats with their stupid earpieces. What's all that about? And why do they always look so threatening? You're just there to open a door, for God's sake – not about to singlehandedly take out a machine-gun nest at Monte Cassino. She's a CUSTOMER, he's a GUEST – get over it! And who's on the end of your earpiece? Heart FM, that's who, not a senior functionary from *Spectre*. Proper, appropriately servile (but never simpering, note) old-school doormen in a proper uniform served a social need, and were almost always ex-services. But the sub-breed that came to infect the species with the explosion in clubs, with their nasty blousons, fascist armbands, shaven heads and sinister expressions are something else altogether. As with all pests, the only sensible solution is extermination.

See also Red ropes outside wannabe in-demand venues

Drizzle

Rain: obviously good, and necessary. Dry weather: often desirable. But anything in between is to be condemned. Makes planning (e.g. days out, what to wear) very tricky, and can look dismal. For pity's sake, do I go out and do the gardening – or not? Easy decision when it's raining/dry, but not when it's something in between. Make your mind up! The French have a word for it – *grisaille* – which just about sums it up.

See also Sleet, Slush

Dropped buttered toast

Yes it's a truism, but has anyone ever dropped a piece of toast and watched it land on the carpet buttered side up? What is all that about?! I remember once being told that the secret of perpetual motion had finally been proven experimentally: you strap a piece of buttered toast to the back of a cat and drop it from the top of a skyscraper – it will keep spinning ad infinitum since a cat always lands on its feet and a slice of toast will always land buttered side

Don't worry darling, kitty will be fine. Daddy's just doing an experiment!

down. Obvious when you think about it, which you will every time you drop a piece of toast from now on.

Dry January

Who first came up with this idea? And who first coined the phrase?! Whoever it was is to be condemned as a heartless, unthinking beast whose cruelty obviously knows no bounds. If there HAS to be a dry month let it be February, mostly on account of its brevity. But preferably, not at all. Maybe switch to a quaffing ale for a couple of days rather than your habitual *morte súbita* or ditch the high-strength Chateau Musar from the sunbaked vineyards of the Bekaa Valley in favour of a light claret from the poorer soils of the northern Medoc. Or simply forget to pack your hip flask from time to time.

See also Movember, Sober for October

Dumbing down

Yes I know, it's a cliché. And you know what I think about clichés. BUT. This is a symptom of our national slide into mediocrity and is to be stoutly resisted at every opportunity. Even most so-called serious documentaries these days repeat their essential proposition at ten-minute intervals – presumably because it is thought our attention span is so short that this is the only way our enfeebled minds can hope to keep track. 'This is the BBC News,' the newsreader will repeat, barely eight minutes after first telling us this amazing fact as the BBC News logo is lovingly dwelt on for the best part of half a minute.

And why those 'amusing' graphics which are aimed at enlightening us about, for example, the Budget?

Or that odd convention whereby a presenter is paid lotsa moolah to stride around against a chroma-key background which to the viewers at home has been designed so that the UK's constituencies have metamorphosed into a series of odd-shaped, different-coloured paving slabs? Please – just show us a neat map, not overly simplified: those excellent chaps at the Ordnance Survey could surely oblige.

Did it all start to go wrong with Martyn Lewis (never trust a chap who spells his name weirdly: St Martin of Tours knew better) and his desire to tack a bit of good news onto the end of serious news bulletins? And maybe it reached its apogee with the light-hearted bits force-fed into *Newsnight* a couple of years ago (though getting their self-important 'highbrow' presenters to do anything inappropriate gets my vote), and now its effects are pervasive almost everywhere you look, making *The Sun*'s leader page of days gone by almost an object lesson in astuteness and enlightened reason.

See also The Proms, The National Trust

E

'Early doors'

Fatuous phrase affected by wannabe northerners who meant to deploy the phrase 'sparrow's fart' to indicate that they'd arisen before dawn.

Elastoplast

Has it ever occurred to the renowned manufacturer of sticking plasters, do you think, that the user might be self-treating and that with a finger on one hand bleeding profusely and inoperable, it will be impossible to peel off those wretched bits of backing tape with one hand? What will happen is, you resort to holding it with your teeth, using them as a clamp, and opening it that way. That inevitably leads to what long-term users refer to as the 'sticking-plaster-doubling-back-on-itself' moment, at which point it is worse than useless. The only thing for it, you realise with resignation, is the old 'twisting-a-bit-of-loo-paper-round-your-finger' technique to staunch the flow of blood. Why the f*ck didn't you do that in the first place?

And in the unlikely event you actually get a bit of plaster stuck down roughly where you want it, there is a grim inevitability that when the time eventually comes to remove it, half of your body hairs will come with it, like a particularly dramatic body-waxing, leaving that bit of fragile bluey-white skin exposed, for all the world like an baby albino hedgehog.

Email strings

Potentially lethal. The object of your ire eleven months ago definitely should not discover that fact accidentally when he's since become your boss, just because a long-forgotten email of yours to a colleague happened to mention in passing that, 'X is such a complete loser – if I had my way I'd have him transferred to our North Korean branch and hope the authorities there quickly work out for themselves that nobody would really notice if he went missing. In fact, if he did, it would probably be a significant, if small, step along the way to total rapprochement with the Kim dynasty.'

Best start an email afresh and not run the risk of being strung up by the string you've long since forgotten and lazily let dangle.

See also Reply to all

Energy saving light bulbs

Almost one and a half centuries after Thomas Edison perfected the modern-day light bulb we now find ourselves travelling in reverse, with the encouragement by governments to buy and use light bulbs which emit nothing more than a faint glow – and a much less aesthetically pleasing one, to boot. Utter nonsense that makes essential activities like reading, completing the crossword and embroidery significantly more difficult, if that's your thing. And the additional irony is, that although they're SUPPOSED to be long-lasting to compensate for the fact that you now need a dozen occasional lamps to provide the light that just a pair of them did before, they are forever self-extinguishing within weeks. Built in bloody obsolescence at work, without a shadow of a doubt – always assuming, of course, that you can generate enough artificial light to produce a shadow worthy of the name.

Estuary English

An unfortunate affected sub-dialect of English speech. Typically adopted by people who are perfectly capable of speaking properly, but for their own reasons choose to seem more what they deem to be a 'man/woman of the people'. Characterised by dropped aitches, glottal stops and phrases like 'y'know…'. Practised and sadly popularised a generation ago by a minor politician by the name of Blair. Couldn't be 'Anthony', could he? 'Nuff said.

Everyone winning on sports day

Does everyone win at The Olympics? Or the Ashes? Or in life? Thought not. That's why the concept of EVERYONE winning on sports day is so thoroughly wrong-headed. Better to invest in thirty-three different rosettes numbered from first to thirty-third than give everyone the same bright red one and the implication that you're all as good as each other at the same things. You're not: get used to it. The little boy who came last in the egg-and-spoon will no doubt turn out to be in a class of his own when it comes to something completely different, like mimicking the voice of their ever-so-slightly weirdo form teacher.

Excruciating rustling

See Rustling

F

F1

See Formula One

Fake candles

What is it with hotels, restaurants, bars etc. that they've caught this disease which embraces the notion that lots of little fake electric candles add ambience? They don't, seriously – they merely serve to irritate. Or as my editor observes, 'they just look shit'. Proper candles can help make for a relaxing ambience in a pub, but even these are being overused – in the same way as the deployment of too many over-elaborate hanging baskets has a way of cumulatively destroying the effect they are striving to achieve (perhaps with the noble exception of the gloriously intemperate plantings covering The Churchill Arms in Notting Hill).

How often do you go into a pub-with-pretensions in the middle of a gloriously sunny day to find dozens of candles burning merrily away, denting the profits and no doubt doubling-up on global warming. It gets on my wick…

Fanny packs

See Bumbags

Fashion

See The fashion industry

Fellow passengers

Oh dear – aren't they AWFUL?! Overly tall ones; overly large ones; plodders; sniffers, suckers and sneezers; dramatic coughers and wheezers; odious ones; elbow-digging ones; hoggers of the armrest; ones with headphones that haven't a sound-reducing feature; loud mobile phone talkers; eaters (especially of hot food); ones with dripping mackintoshes; ones across a train-table from you who don't understand the concept of shared foot space; back in the day, people who hadn't yet learned how to turn the pages of a broadsheet newspaper without causing the person next to them physical injury (actually, you know, I rather miss that); air passengers who spend ten minutes, it sometimes seems, standing in the aisle making a meal out of putting items in the overhead locker as well as small talk, whilst a hundred more others jostle on the aircraft steps.

Travel tends to make a misanthropist of me – but given the above (and more), is that REALLY so surprising?!

See also Amateur fellow travellers, Bumbags, Rucksacks

Film sequels and overexposed TV series

Was there EVER a good one except *Naked Gun 2½*? Nope. I mean – was there an *Easy Rider 2* or *Bullitt #2*? Hey – the rule is simple. If it becomes a franchise it invariably becomes a pile of toss. Oh, and remakes: WHY, for pity's sake?! Isn't ONE version of *The ABC Murders* enough to last a lifetime? But at least it's a bit late to remake *2001: A Space Odyssey*, though I suppose you could make a case for a more…erm…contemporary take on *Seven Brides for Seven Brothers*, but 'Seven Messy Relationships

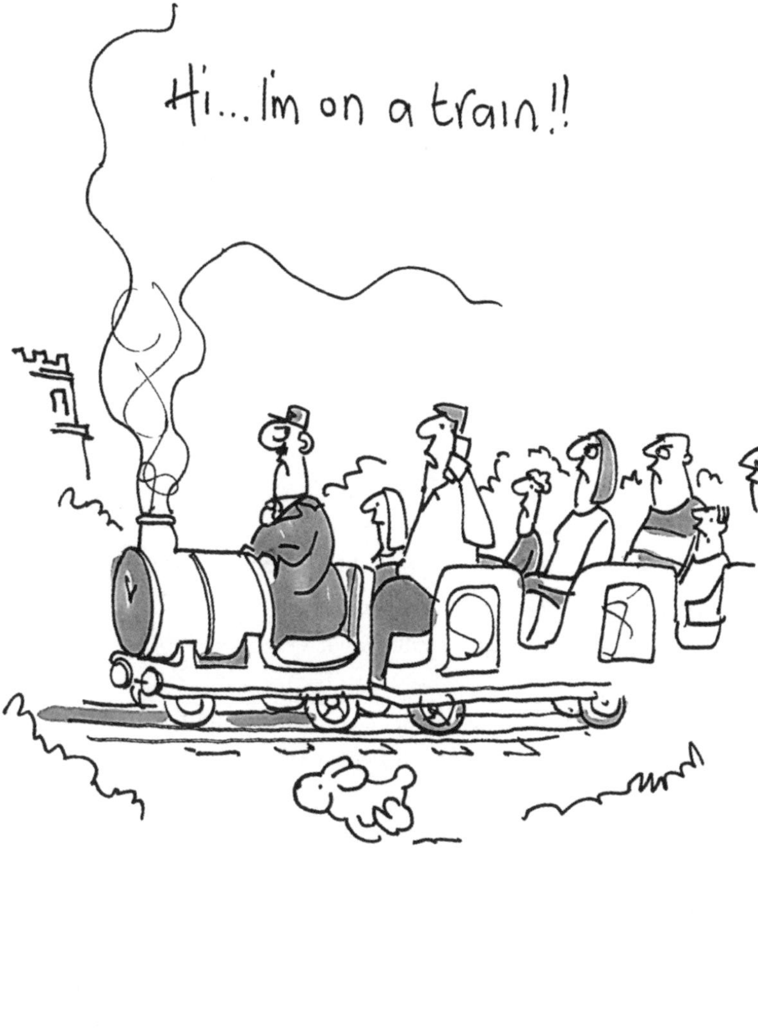
Hi... I'm on a train!!

for Seven Confused Brothers, Lovers, Significant Others, Exes and Absent Fathers Etc.' doesn't trip off the tongue quite so easily.

Flashing images

Don't you get sick of hearing on almost every TV news bulletin 'and I should warn you that this report contains some flashing images'? Is that REALLY necessary? And did you know that a whole new industry has sprung up on the back of a gentleman named Harding who suggested that flashing images, strobing etc. of a certain kind has been known to trigger epileptic fits? And guess what: who invented the machine that can predict this, and for a fee will tell you?

Flossing

(Not to be confused with the absurd dance move that was briefly fashionable some years back.) Why do dental hygienists – a relatively new trade – talk down to you as if you were a recalcitrant nine-year-old behaving badly in class? Don't they know that the jury is very much out on flossing? It's not just that it hurts, is tedious and time-consuming or has a name that makes it sound frivolous. They really should keep up with the science on this. The US health department has dropped its recommendation for daily flossing; Public Health England is – as the parlance has it – monitoring the situation; and some at the British Dental Association say it is largely ineffective. And yet, every time one goes to the dentist, he or his assistant will make a great show of twisting bits of thread around their fingers, before working it vigorously between all one's teeth one by one, purely with the aim, it seems, of drawing as much precious blood as possible and inducing yelps of pain, in the process extending the length of the appointment which inevitably increases its cost. It doesn't take much of a conspiracy theorist to make the connection.

Formula One

A long time ago, this was an exciting motorsport in which daring young men risked their lives racing against each other in very noisy, very powerful cars, powered by proper engines devouring proper petrol. Now reduced to the dismal spectacle of a small number of young men following each other in small, quiet cars in a tedious, orderly procession around a racetrack that has been carefully designed to remove all traces of excitement (e.g. the possibility of overtaking, crashing etc.) and make it as far distant as possible from spectators. As if this weren't enough, highly complex rules have also been devised to eliminate every other possibility of risk or competition, such as winning by beating other cars in a race. Without a shadow of doubt these days are a waste of too much of a precious weekend.

French workers

See All French workers

Fruit with meat

An abomination. I don't care if it's called a tagine and they enjoy it in some parts of the world, it's just WRONG – especially as so often the fruity bits outnumber the meaty ones. I was once served a pub roast – the usual thing, two thick slices of overcooked beef with the consistency of tarmac – where the chef (no doubt trying to be adventurous) had plonked a few slices of strawberry, of all things, on the side of the plate, with thick gravy lapping at them. What was already a deeply unsatisfactory experience was instantly and unnecessarily transformed into a thoroughly disturbing one. And, pray, where did the tradition of the piece of gammon wilfully polluted with a slice of pineapple originate, or the pizza garnished with all manner of un-Italian foreign objects (chicken tikka, anyone?!)? It must have been during the same era as someone invented the upended-half-a-melon covered in cocktail sticks, porcupine-style, bearing little knobs of Cheddar cheese and silverskin onions. The sixties have a lot to answer for, what with these, inner ring roads, avocado bathroom suites and mass tourism, to name but a few.

Fusion food

Why?! Polish – good. Chinese – good. But Polish/Chinese, Mexican/Thai, Peruvian/Vietnamese? A tiresome affectation designed to get a new restaurant noticed, with zero likelihood of being sustained beyond its launch period. CAMOUFLAGED fusion food, on the other hand, seems to work well: I give you almost every single curry house in the country. Here, what passes for Indian fare bears as much relation to the real thing as one of those pub walls lined with stuck-on book backs does to a real library. There's a posh phrase for it: 'anglicised ethnicity'. You heard it here first. Probably.

See also All-purpose oriental restaurants, Fruit with meat

G

Gatwick Airport

Don't go there.

Generalisations

Seldom if ever justified, unless I make them.

Glue that sticks to everything but what you want it to

So. You've managed to extricate your expensive little tube of superglue from its near-impenetrable packaging. Pause for small smile of self-satisfaction, shortly to be replaced (you already know this, don't you?) by the familiar grimace of dismay – because now comes the fun of piercing the cap and screwing the impossibly small spreader back into place without smearing superglue all over your fingers. That won't happen: you knew that before you even bought the damned thing in the first place. What happens is that for days to come you will have no sensation in your fingertips whatsoever because there's a dense unremovable layer of hardened adhesive where once your fingerprints resided.

'Aha!' you think, trying to be positive – but there's just enough freedom of movement left in your hands to squirt a tiny bit of glue onto the broken thing that you were optimistically trying to fix in the first place. But it's not going to work, is it? You'll just end up with two broken bits of whatever, each coated with a couple of quid's worth of superglue that's already gone rock hard and will never come together properly again. And which are now stuck fast to your hands. Just bin it, for pity's sake. Oh, and the barely used tube of superglue as well, because experience tells you that the little spreader will never again permit a molecule of glue to escape the tube: it's already stuck completely fast – for eternity, rather like your index finger and the next one along, that used to be just close friends but are now completely conjoined, Siamese-twin-style.

And as for Araldite – don't get me started! It's just like all the above, but even more expensive, with TWO different tubes that you're supposed to mix together (by what, in what, I'd like to know) to create an apparently hyper-efficient adhesive. But when you come back to it weeks later, for a second attempt on the same job that inevitably didn't work first time around, you'll find that the caps are stuck fast to the tubes, which means slicing the top off each to get at the gloop inside. And you know what that means, don't you? Yep, another week of unusable fingertips and bits of glue just where you most didn't want them – furniture, clothing, carpet – that will be impossible to eradicate. And nothing short of napalm will sort that – trust me.

'Go large'

Phrase promoted by McDonald's restaurants to describe a meal consisting of larger portions. It is not merely accurately descriptive but self-fulfilling in the sense that buyers who take this option obviously…go large themselves. It is also a constant source of irritation for those who carefully specify a Big Mac Meal, for example, at the counter, to be instantly countered with the extra sales-incentivised question, 'Do you want to go large?' The answer which is staring you in the face is, 'If I'd wanted to "go large" I would obviously have stated that choice in the first place, but since I try to be careful of my appearance and wellbeing I forbear to do any such thing.'

In the event, with grim inevitability, you merely say, 'No thank you', and realise anew that, whilst consistency might be a virtue, predictability seldom is.

Golf, golfers, golfing clothes, golf clubs

Oh dear. Golf courses obviously inhibit the gobbling-up of green spaces by hideous retail parks and unlovely housing developments, but beyond that it is hard to see any obvious

advantage to anything connected with golf. However hard they try, it DOESN'T make for good television. ('Ooooh', said in a slightly sub-sexual way too close to the microphone doesn't do it for me, I don't know about you, any more than does the phrase 'that's a beauty', spoken admiringly to a small white ball that has just landed a mere thirty metres from the flag on the lip of a bunker.) Golfers themselves, of course, are simply beyond the pale – and not just because of the horrendous outfits they tend to sport. As far as I can make out, most of them are off-duty taxi drivers, simply waiting for the opportunity to transfer their habitual road rage to any walker who strays too close to the bit of rustic rough they had their eye on as a likely landing-place for their next shot. This, inevitably, is merely a precursor to a lengthy sojourn in the clubhouse, as like as not some 1970s interpretation of an imagined New England Country Club in the English suburbs, festooned with signs saying things like 'Reserved for the Lady Captain'. Yuk.

See also Formula One

Guessing the wrong platform
when arriving at a station

Can there be anything more profoundly irritating to the long-suffering professional commuter than standing by the door on the wrong side of the carriage while less seasoned travellers with no forethought whatsoever are set to be first off? (Well, yes there can, obviously, ibid, passim etc. etc.) We've all tried to hedge our bets by standing middle-ish in the grubby bit of the carriage between the two doors, and hoping that no one sneaks past to gain provisional pole position, but there's always someone who's alert to your tactics and relishing the resulting psychological warfare. By contrast, guessing and getting it right provides one of the few glimmers of hope that the day ahead might not be all bad after all.

It works – or rather, doesn't – the other way around as well. If you've ever had the misfortune to be stranded at Basingstoke station you'll know what I mean. Deep in your soul, although the tannoy is continually telling you that the next train to Salisbury will depart from platform two, you KNOW that it will depart from platform one. But, meek spirit that you are, you loiter on platform two, more in hope than expectation, and then at the last moment as the anonymous voice changes its mind, you charge down the ramp with 3000 other desperate west-heading commuters, secure in the knowledge that all hope of securing a seat left with your risible gullibility.

H

Hairdressing salon names that try to be amusing but aren't

In amongst all the shocking puns so often deployed in this sector, one that made me laugh for its inventiveness as well as inappropriateness (wrong country) was 'Estu'hair' on the banks of the Gironde estuary in southwest France. And they're FRENCH! Most are, of course, simply dreadful. What IS it about hairdressers that see a need to distinguish their establishments with an unfunny name? Butchers as a rule don't, neither do fishmongers nor greengrocers.

I mean…'The 2nd Combing', 'Sheer Elegance', 'Hair It Is', 'Hair's Looking At You' and the truly ghastly 'Sheerlock Combs'. I sometimes wonder if there's a retired copywriter out there who cut his teeth on ancient hair product ads and who has struck a rich seam of gold wandering around the Western world, using the name 'Puns 'r' Us', hawking his wares from a portfolio of mind-numbingly bad-pun names that he's been building up tirelessly since the mid-sixties. Whatever, there should definitely be a section for this category alone at advertising awards ceremonies, with the winner taking home a plausible gilt imitation of a half-filled sick bag.

See also Puns, Tattoos

Half-in/half-out Rawlplugs

Unused Rawlplugs – good. Rawlplugs safely in their carefully drilled hole – good. But any halfway house? Nothing short of disastrous. It's no good getting out your hammer and trying to bash it in: all that will happen is that you will damage the wall, bend the Rawlplug irreparably, and permanently close the hole that might be of use if you ever manage to extricate it in its entirety and salvage it for future use. Which, as a matter of record, you will not be able to do. Your only solution is to snip away at the sticky-out bit with a pair of pincers or Stanley knife and then smear Polyfilla all over it. For the rest of your days there will then be an ugly bump on an otherwise smooth surface to remind you not just of your incompetence but why DIY is such a fool's errand in the first place.

Hand dryers

First, there were individual hand towels in conveniences, respectfully proffered to you by a uniformed attendant. Then came the blight of the long thin towel on a roller which jammed stuck on every third tug and started to tear during its first morning of usage. Then, paper 'towelettes'. Following these emerged the warm hand blower, generally activated by pressing a button that wafted a not-unenjoyable gentle mild breeze over your hands. Hot on its heels, almost literally, came the blower which self-activated when you waved your hand under its all-seeing eye. This, typically, had a moveable nozzle which theoretically tilted this way and that, permitting the drying of other parts of one's anatomy. The fatal flaw of this, however, was that it cut out the second you tilted it, and so was useless. Or 'not fit for purpose' as modern-day types have it.

Then along came Mr Dyson and a host of imitators, who devised a way of producing a powerful directional blast of air from a lethal-looking machine, with almost as much thrust as is produced by a fully loaded Harrier Jump Jet taking off

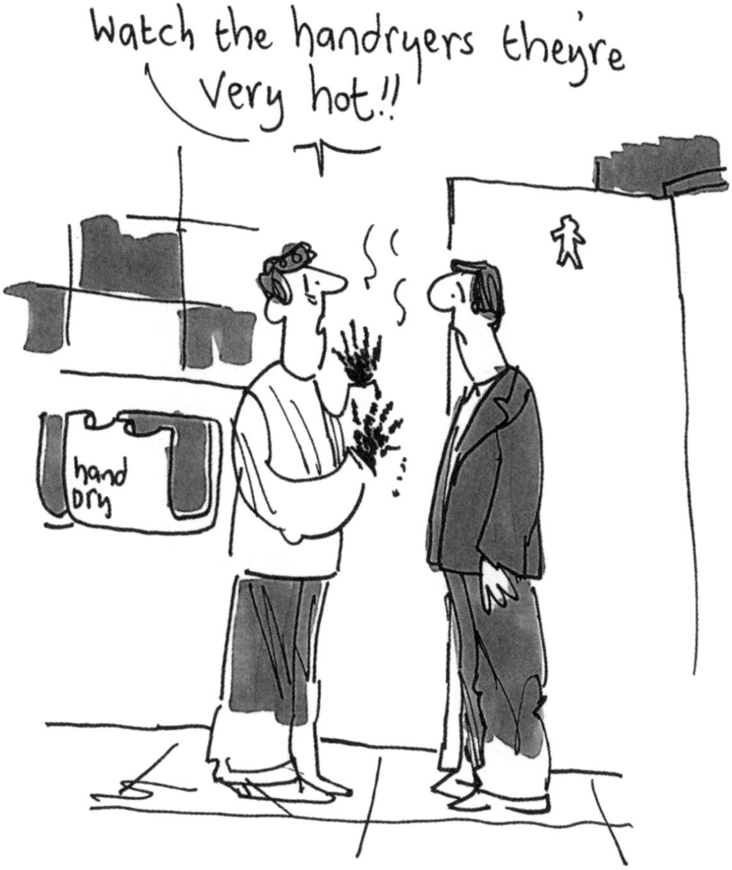
Watch the handryers they're very hot!!
hand dry

a bit sharpish. This cannot dry your hands, or anything else, but produces so much noise that everyone in the restaurant two closed doors away KNOWS when you emerge from the washrooms THAT YOU HAVE WASHED YOUR HANDS. They're still damp, of course, but you've done the decent thing.

Hashtags

#alwaystiresome. Obviously.
Strongly imply #jumpingonbandwagons
and #tediousselfpublicity, so as such are to be deplored.

Their first appearance in the current usage can be dated to mid-2007, and now there are even websites dedicated to them. But to most civilised people they surely are better known as a 'sharp' – as in F sharp, probably the first used by most musicians in the scale of G major. It is ironic that most tweets employing a hashtag are in fact anything but sharp.

If you wish to be further confused, the symbol itself is called in some societies a 'hash'; in the US it's known as a pound sign (don't ask; what do they know?); but technically is properly named an octothorpe. Whatever – let's just agree that the world – and not just Twitter or Instagram – would be a happier place without an infestation of hashtags.

Health & Safety

'A wonderful thing is the Board of Trade. Before, there wasn't any Board, and now there isn't any trade.' This slight misquotation from the wonderfully prescient A.P. Herbert has an obvious parallel to the health & safety industry or lobby (more like). This concept, probably first 'concretised' in the mid-seventies, has come to define pretty much everything that is bad and seedy in contemporary Britain. As a consequence, for example, pavements have apparently become death traps, car parks little better than minefields, and butchers' shops the sort of places that might give Hannibal Lecter pause to reconsider his vocation. Why can't I walk/park/eat/cook/drink/have sex here? PLEASE! Back will come the inevitable, sadly rhetorical answer: 'It's 'ealth an' safety, innit?' A bit like Fortnum & Mason, Bonnie & Clyde or Parsley & Thyme, these two in themselves perfectly workmanlike words have been conjoined to form a terrifying and alien force, before which we all quake. Stuff & Nonsense, as earlier generations would have matter-of-factly retorted.

See also Personnel, Nannying

Hen parties

Back in the day, I might have quietly fantasised about leaping out of a giant cake at a hen party and being inappropriately molested by a bunch of tiddly bridesmaids-to-be. But no longer. With their ghastly shrieking, vile cocktails, matching T-shirts, pink cowboy hats, naff sashes and all manner of phallic-themed items, hen parties are definitely to be avoided at all costs. They're even capable of blighting such places as Bournemouth, Brighton and Luton Airport – and that takes some doing – and by all accounts can sometimes last for the best part of a week, during which time any unsuspecting halfway-reasonable-looking bloke the party comes across is likely to be left a gibbering wreck, stripped of his dignity and almost certainly much more besides.

See also Stag weekends

High-waisted trousers

What gets into men of a certain age and status that they suddenly feel the need to don trousers the waistline of which brushes against the nipples? It always reminds me of Tweedledum and Tweedledee, or Humpty Dumpty: why DO they do it?! It only draws attention to the fact that they can't have seen their wedding tackle in eons except in the reflection from a mirrored floor.

'Holds knife like pen' (HKLP)

Unacceptable behaviour under any circumstances, both on account of its uncouthness and impracticality. Hey, there's a lot of Victorian nonsense about table manners that's best consigned to the social history books, but this is one faux pas too far even for a generation brought up to graze rather than dine.

See also Shovel action by people eating

Holding patterns
(esp. Gatwick on a Monday morning)

It should be SO simple. You draw a straight line from, for example, Barcelona to London Gatwick and you follow it. There's really no need for those endless spirals that someone's drawn on the end. You know the score: you circle endlessly, with the sun blinding you every 240 degrees, and you get to see Horsham for the umpteenth time, when all you want to do is get off, dash for the Gatwick Express and make it to your desk before anyone notices you've been away for ANOTHER long weekend. And it's already a full thirty minutes since the wretched pilot first uttered the immortal – and obviously hopelessly optimistic – phrase, 'Cabin crew, prepare for landing.' So not fun.

See also Gatwick Airport

Hospitality industry

Sorry, but how can serving a few drinks and canapés or making beds in a hotel be termed an industry? It's a trade. Get over it. Industry implies real work – not poncing about in a pinny or pivoting with a plate of nibbles. Puhlease.

See also The fashion industry

Hospitality suite(s)

Vile descriptor, vile place(s). Typically contains a group of unsober, inappropriately attired men with their backs firmly turned to whatever it is everybody else in the vicinity is paying good money – THEIR OWN money! – to watch. A third-rate luncheon is normally followed by an extremely poor coffee-type beverage served way too hot and too weak, to be followed soon after by tea served from a similar container and smelling/ tasting remarkably like the aforementioned coffee.

Hotel room doors

Let's be clear: as a hotel guest, all you really need is a door to your room that locks – and a key that locks/unlocks it. So why has a whole industry crept up on us unawares, developing ever-more fiendish devices that make this seemingly simple process near impossible to accomplish? There are plastic cards which supposedly work by touching a device on the outside of the door, or maybe to one side. There are plastic cards which you have to insert in the locking apparatus, though which way up or round is never made clear. There are fob-like objects. I could go on.

But the one thing all these irritating items have in common is that they will almost certainly not work WHEN YOU MOST WANT THEM TO: you're outside your room and desperate for a pee, or you can hear your phone ringing inside the room and you can't get to it. Whatever, you'd feel better about it if it wasn't so damn predictable.

And of course – IT'S YOUR FAULT. Obviously. Apparently, you've thoroughly irresponsibly kept it in the same pocket as your phone – which you now are told kills it stone dead. Now, if you've been concentrating, you will recall that one of the scenarios above has your phone IN THE ROOM, separated from the plastic key by, among other things, a locked door. Try explaining this, rationally, to the hotel receptionist, and see the response you will get.

No actually, on the other hand, don't bother: just meekly accept the criticism and the replacement plastic card. And brace yourself for the upcoming battle with the light switches and the shower, suitably fortified, I suggest, with something small, strong and inevitably pricey from the minibar.

See also Hotel rooms with incomprehensible light switches, Showers that are impossible to work, Taps/plugs that don't work

Hotel rooms with incomprehensible
light switches

It is axiomatic that, the more expensive the hotel, the less likely you are to be able to work any of the switches in your room. There will be some that work the windows, for example...the blinds...the main light...the bedside lights...the table lamp...the lights in the bathroom...and so on ad tedium. None, of course, will work in any conceivably rational way – if at all.

Ever. You will probably try putting the plastic room key into a slot next to the door, almost inevitably the wrong way up/round, but still nothing happens. In the end, you have no choice but to summon the concierge to explain everything – in the full knowledge that this might work in the middle of the afternoon with him present, but there's absolutely no chance of getting the lights to work at 11 p.m. when you're back with a skinful and most need them.

It is of course the same with the television in your hotel room. No matter that in the course of your adult life you've owned or used dozens of different brands of TV and remote control, and fancy yourself as a bit of a gadget-freak: the one confronting you now has no obvious means of operation. No visible switches. No plug. No little green/red light as a giveaway. No nothing. And a remote control that might have been left by a previous guest from a previous visit to a different hotel, for all the use it is. Give up, and go and watch the footie on a big telly in the bar downstairs, even if you will be surrounded by lager-swilling oiks of the more appalling kind. Life's too short.

See also Hotel room doors, Showers that are impossible to work

Hyper-parenting

Listen. Little Johnny is NOT going to die of sunstroke and/ or melanoma after ten minutes' exposure to a few moments' sunshine on a hazy afternoon in Llandudno, so there's absolutely no reason to smother him in factor 50 before zipping him up in the kind of wetsuit more suited to extreme surfing conditions in midwinter. He's more likely to suffer from vitamin D deficiency and soon start displaying the unpleasant symptoms of rickets! Let the little blighter run around in his birthday suit for an hour for God's sake or splash about naked in the paddling pool.

And don't insist that he/she counts their ten tables backwards while they're at it: children need time to CHILL. Too many hobbies, too many activities, too many before- and after-school clubs, too many frenetic online/on-tablet activities – no wonder half the population appears to suffer from Attention Deficit Hyperactivity Disorder, unlike such excellent role models for an earlier generation as Richmal Crompton's William Brown.

And as for 'helicopter parenting' – so called because the parents continually hover over their children, even when supposedly in loco parentis at school – for God's sake get a sense of perspective. What did someone once famously say? 'I like children but I couldn't eat a whole one': maybe a bit inappropriate, but you get the gist.

Ice in whisky

An abomination. Not to be confused with ice in *whiskey*, which is de rigueur, obviously, unless it's Irish. It should go without saying that good Scotch whisky should be tempered with the addition of the same quantity of cool, high-quality water. Er, that's it. Any barman who believes otherwise should be given his marching orders with immediate effect: God knows I've tried.

Inappropriate spending by government, national, regional and local bodies

Potholes: tick. Schools: tick. Streetlights: tick: Rubbish collection: tick. Defence of the Realm: tick. Lollypop ladies: tick. Er, that's about it, isn't it?

All that wretched propaganda (local news-sheets, natch)… consultancy…steering groups…support groups…health & safety nonsense…ad bloody nauseam should all be binned. But only fortnightly, obviously, and only in the dark blue bins not the green, brown or grey ones, otherwise you'll be fined and your credit rating might be affected.

One might have hoped that this interference by government in tasks which are clearly non-governmental would have started to die out with the disappearance of Red Ted of Lambeth fame… and maybe hastened by 'the cuts' and the recent dominance of centre-right parties. But no, not a bit of it. Worse, when they DO spend our money on stuff that makes sense, they balls it up. Like building aircraft carriers that cost three times what they should, leak copiously, and have no aircraft on them. Or railway lines that cost half of our entire GDP and will be redundant before they're finished because by then everyone will be teleporting or some such (and do we REALLY want the Midlands to be fifteen minutes closer to London?).

Inappropriate/out-of-context tat

Did it all start with those shelves full of unwanted, probably unread second-hand books lining the walls of otherwise perfectly inoffensive pubs? By all means stick a few framed photographs/prints/maps of the area on the walls – and maybe a saucy picture on the wall above the urinal – but why pile loads of old jugs, crockery, farm implements, discarded clothing etc. in the corners of just about every hostelry in the country? It's all in the name of ambience, I suppose, but don't these people realise that artificially concocted ambience is invariably worse than no ambience whatsoever?

The same goes for restaurants with framed, signed pictures of 'celebrities' who've clearly never been within a million miles of the place. I mean – who WOULD? Even in the sixties, when most of these seem to date from. What makes it even worse is that the chisel-jawed man with the brilliantined hair in that photograph wasn't even famous then – over half a century ago. AND the signature's probably fake.

Incompetent cocktail barmen

It's all very well, all that tossing of bottles and cocktail shakers, pouring drinks from a great height or from behind your back –

but please Mr Wannabe World-class Cocktail Barman, just mix me a halfway-decent Negroni in less than the time it takes to recite *Gunga Din*. Slowly. What is with all that performance when it is only the ingredients, their proportions and temperature, and the style of glass that really matter?

PLEASE don't serve a Bloody Mary that's got a blasted green olive lurking in it and a block of ice so big it might just have been carved from the Antarctic shelf. You simply need a tallish glass, some tomato juice, vodka, dry sherry, horseradish, salt, pepper, garlic salt, Tabasco, Lea & Perrins Worcestershire Sauce, a stick of celery and a small quantity of ice. Maybe a discreet slice of lemon – oh, and another shot of vodka for luck. There is no earthly reason why this should take more than one and a half minutes to concoct and serve. Thank you.

If in doubt, take my tip and always order two cocktails simultaneously: it will save an inordinate amount of time queuing for the second, and having to watch the wretched guy go through his histrionics a second time.

See also Ice in whisky

Instant coffee

Yes, it's instant. No, it's not coffee. Yuk. The only resemblance it bears to coffee is its colour and the fact that it's hot. It should therefore be marketed as 'Instant brown liquid-maker that can be served hot and may in an emergency be drunk', to avoid the possibility of causing confusion amongst less-informed consumers.

Intrusive noise

Right. You're sitting in the laughably named 'quiet carriage' when a booming voice over the public address system shouts that 'YOU WILL FIND THE QUIET COMPARTMENTS SITUATED IN THE THIRD AND SIXTH CARRIAGES OF THIS SIX-COACH TRAIN!!!' Not so quiet now, is it? Or you can be walking along a moving pavement, quietly minding your own business when another invisible voice warns you, 'YOU ARE APPROACHING THE END OF THE CONVEYOR!!!!! START WALKING NOW!!!!!!!!!!!!!' Dear lord, if it's THAT lethal maybe it should be uninstalled instantly.

See also Health & Safety, Nannying

Jet skis

Noisy, nasty, naff, a nuisance and nearly always being ridden by ne'er-do-wells.

See also Alliteration

K

'Keep calm and...'

Clever and appropriate in its original manifestation. Mildly amusing in the first days of its 'second coming'. Now merely tedious because of its omnipresence and many unfunny usages. Guaranteed to have the opposite effect to the original command, i.e. make one ANYTHING but calm.

See also Visual clichés

Kid-centric

Let's not pussyfoot around – this is a completely unacceptable philosophy so far as the management of family life or community generally is concerned. And not just because of the word 'kid': 'child-centric' would only be a marginal improvement on something that at heart cannot be improved upon. Adults know stuff, children don't. QED.

See also Kidults

Kidults

Grow up! If you're old enough to vote, you're old enough to stop playing computer games, skateboard, and spend all your time at home (and in many cases down the shops) slobbing around in your 'jamas. And while I'm at it, please don't address me as 'bro': even my bros don't do that.

L

Lampshades that don't sit right

(i) It is an immutable law of civilised living that the base of a lampshade should be exactly horizontal and not sloppily askew. Any other angle is guaranteed to disturb one's equilibrium and may even trigger migraines, or worse, an epileptic fit.

(ii) It is, however, equally an immutable law of product design that every known contraption for holding a lampshade is highly likely to make every attempt to follow rule (i) above doomed to failure.

No one has yet managed to square this circle and so those of us who care about such things are resigned to having to straighten every lampshade every single time the lights are switched on. A tiresome but necessary chore, sadly.

Lazy dog owners

I've had dogs for decades, yet I am as averse to the mess they can leave behind as much as the most fastidious of pet-haters. It's simple: if your dog performs in public, clear the bloody stuff up! And make it easier on yourself by feeding the mutt on dry dogfood not slops, and certainly not anything containing prunes, grapes or muesli. As a dog owner, perhaps the thing I most hate is mowing the lawn on a beautiful spring day and having the scent of fresh-cut grass polluted with mashed-up, hi-fibre dog turd. Get a shovel and flick it, golfball-out-of-a-bunker-style, into your detested neighbour's pristine back garden – that way at least there's a small compensatory smirk to be had. Unless you get caught in the act (I've been there…).

The only amusing incident in this connection that I can recall is one of our dogs once 'straining at stool' and with an anguished yelp eventually emitting one of a neighbour's daughter's knee-length white socks from its nether extremity. That's retrievers for you. All other doggie-doo anecdotes are vile pretty much by definition: on which note, is there any behavioural tic more appalling than a dog owner collecting the 'output' from their pet in a small black plastic bag and then hanging it from a tree for all the world like a homespun Scandinavian Christmas tree decoration? You can almost begin to understand the mentality that drives some to set the stuff on fire and ram it through an unfriendly acquaintance's letterbox. Almost.

Listicles

Mostly tedious (e.g. as 'clickbait'), especially when used as publicity-seeking devices, unless made by me, or devised with some useful purpose in mind (e.g. shopping lists, to-do lists, people-I'd-like-to-see-dead lists). For pity's sake deliver us from the likes of the Top Ten Wardrobe Malfunctions Of All Time and Celebrities That Haven't Aged Well.

See also Generalisations

Loo rolls

See New loo rolls with the end stuck down, Loo rolls in public conveniences

Loo rolls in public conveniences

Only someone with a truly evil sense of humour can have invented those loo paper dispensers that consist of a large, semi-hidden roller locked away behind a cover, whose sole aim in life is to prevent anyone getting at the very product it is designed to serve. You know the scenario: the time has come to tear a few pieces off, but the bit that should be dangling from it is nowhere to be seen. In as unhygienic a manner as is possible to conceive, you work your hand into the contraption, trying to get it to spin and disgorge its precious cargo. First of all, of course, it refuses to budge, whilst tantalisingly – yearningly, even – you can see positively miles of pristine loo paper through a semi-transparent window. Then, suddenly, it starts to spin energetically, stirring all kinds of positive emotions in your breast (and elsewhere, probably), but then still refuses to produce the critical end-piece that will enable you to pull a few pieces free.

There's nothing else for it now. Half hitching your trousers up, you unlock the door, hoping against hope that no one else is around, and then you hop into the next cubicle, where THIS version of the infernal machine is displaying its wares in such a way that you can actually grab a sheet. The relief!

And then, finally, on the way out, you pass the machine displaying big, backlit buttons showing the spectrum of faces from red/angry to green/smiley, inviting you to evaluate your experience. With what glee do you thump the red one so hard that it cracks! It was probably heading that way anyway, through extreme overuse: I mean – does anyone ever tap the smiley face button denoting a highly pleasurable public toilet experience? Pervert.

Loud eating

Why do people feel the need to consume vast quantities of food the moment they enter a cinema? The consumption of alcohol – QUIETLY – in there is clearly to be encouraged. But – eating? Noisily? There can be hardly an activity known to man more likely to induce nausea and disgust. I've always supposed it to be the case that the foods on sale in the foyers of cinemas have been especially selected for their decibel potential – the crunching of crisps, the slurping of ice cream, the noisome straw-sucking of a Kia-Ora, the endless munching of popcorn – ad nauseam. If people MUST keep their hunger pangs at bay couldn't they either just temporarily vacate the premises or stick to a small Tupperware of, for example, chilled consommé (cold to minimise the possibility of odours), delicately and silently sipped with the aid of a soup spoon, carried for the purpose?

And all you people who persist in walking and eating simultaneously. Can you REALLY be so busy that your day doesn't permit just a few minutes to sit somewhere appropriate and eat whatever portable food you are lugging around at rest, rather than when you are traipsing around? Actually, in a sense it is probably oxymoronic, in that people who walk and eat simultaneously almost invariably look the most likely to have time on their hands... But of course, all these misdemeanours fade into insignificance compared with the heinous offence of chomping at a decibel on a par with Deep Purple at their loudest. You would think that few human activities would be simpler to impart and to learn than the business of putting food in one's mouth and then closing it before starting to masticate. But judging from the near-universality of the failure to grasp this elementary lesson, its difficulty must be up there with tying shoelaces (especially those wretched, thin slippery ones that typically adorn deck shoes); cutting the fingernails of your right hand if you're right-handed; and Einstein's general theory of relativity.

A potato crisp does NOT need to be smashed to smithereens between your front teeth whilst your mouth gapes open: wait till it's closed. Slurping is NOT an attractive behavioural tic. And lip-smacking noises might signify appreciation of what you're eating in some cultures, but surely not in any that has a pretence to being civilised.

See also People who don't watch where they're going when they're looking at their mobile phone

Loud keyboard usage

On most devices, you can reduce/eliminate the noise of fingers on a keyboard. And you should, if you're using this in a public space. And whatever your sex, please keep the length of your fingernails to a sensible length, since this will also help reduce keyboard clatter. Have you noticed how this truly horrific noise pollution even persists above the sound of the most persistent of public address systems on your train?

See also People who confuse the concepts of 'working' and 'being at work'

Loud mobile phone calls

It's OK, you're not speaking into a tin can linked to another by a length of string: you don't need to raise your voice. And no, we're not interested in what you have to say in the first place. So please, if you must talk on your mobile phone in our earshot, speak quietly and briefly…or mostly listen. Or both. Thank you.

Loud/unamusing ringtones on mobile phones

Why does it need to ring loudly? Especially in a public space, where your mobile phone is likely to be inches from you. So, it's simple: reduce the volume (pretty please). And at the same time bear in mind that a ringtone which you find amusing/entertaining/inventive might sound simply irritating to others. Play it in the confines of your bedroom, not at full volume on the 18.14 to Clapham Junction.

M

Malls

The Mall is clearly a good thing. Pall Mall is a fairly good thing. Everything else with the word 'mall' attached is very definitely not – especially shopping malls. Apparently they like this kind of thing in places like America and Dubai – but that doesn't mean we need to have them plonked down willy-nilly across the UK. The rot started with things like the Arndale Centre and the Brent Cross Shopping Centre, decades ago, and has unfortunately spread the length and breadth of the country. They are singularly unlovely and in their ubiquity have of course contributed to the sad decline of the British town centre.

See also Atonal music

Man flu

Demeaning, dismissive name given by females (esp. mothers-in-law and already-unhappy wives) to the illness involving a raised temperature, bunged-up nose, sore throat and loss of libido which occasionally afflicts otherwise hale and hearty blokes. The last laugh, however, is on the female of the species, since the newest research suggests that a difference between the M/F immune systems may be playing a part in generating this hitherto laughed at affliction.

Not to be confused, obviously, with 'wine-flu', a very real and deadly serious ailment typically manifesting itself on Saturday/Sunday/Monday mornings. Symptoms include sweating, headaches, pronounced trembling and an obsession with having a full English. Causes unknown. The French, interestingly, have a phrase for it, despite the fact that all they drink these days is Badoit. '*Gueule de bois*' is thought to come about from having been *totalement beurre* the night before. Recovery periods amongst Frenchmen are hampered by the general unavailability of a full English and the impractical journey time to the nearest Greggs.

Merlot

Girly grape type which is sadly increasingly included by winemakers in their products to make proper red wines more 'approachable'. If wines weren't so soft and easy-drinking, maybe people wouldn't drink them in quite such absurdly large quantities, our town centres wouldn't be quite so vile in the evening and our casualty centres less pressurised. One should have to WORK to appreciate wine, in the same way that enjoying mustard and whisky didn't come naturally in one's late teens.

See also Wine descriptions

Middle managers

Does anyone have any idea what a middle manager is or does? All offices containing more than, say, a dozen staff seem to have one – or in some cases, hundreds – all beavering busily away... but at what? Male versions are normally identifiable by their bad taste in clothing and bad teeth, and their unmistakeable sense of self-importance. The bungalow they inevitably retreat to once they've taken early retirement (they ALWAYS take early retirement, it goes without saying, rather than 'being let go') will almost certainly bear a pottery nameplate that says 'Duntimeservin' with a small graphic of a cluster of biros and one of those devices that removes staples. Back in the day they'd have had a breast pocket stuffed with pencils, pens and erasers and likely have stuffed their shirt into their underpants. These days it'll be a uniform of M&S's evergreen 'Under-Manager' range.

Female versions tend to be short-haired, sporting severe glasses and wearing sensible shoes. Do they still have one of those spikes on their desk on which slips of paper are aggressively mounted, accompanied with a dramatic harrumph? I do hope so. These days their computer screens will be partially covered with fading Post-it notes, and the wall behind it will carry motivational statements such as 'Do it Now' and 'You don't have to be mad to work here, but it helps'. The first is ironic, obviously, in her case, and the second merely honest.

But what do they DO, these middle managers? As far as anyone can make out, their role is to impede any kind of progress that an individual or the organisation itself might conceivably make. They have a thousand ways of saying NO, and their tools are obfuscation, procrastination, a faked deference to the powers-that-be, and an impenetrable language peculiar to the species, stuffed full with obscure acronyms and cod business-speak. By the way, you know when you're of no interest to the business in which you work when you find yourself intentionally marooned next to one of these types at the office Christmas do, getting morosely pissed on warm white wine: you'll vow to look for a new job at the start of the New Year. It's senior management's adroit way of easing you out – death through a thousand yawns

– without having to expensively resort to bloody HR best practice.

See also Business jargon, Acronyms

Midges (and other pointless insects)

Utterly horrid and pointless, with the capacity to cause annoyance and harm out of all proportion to their size. I read somewhere that in 2018 some long-suffering midge counter estimated Scotland had 68 billion of the beasts hatching by the mid-year point (HOW DID HE KNOW? They never sit still long enough to be counted in my experience, unless they're sitting on my forearm). Can you IMAGINE?!

See also Mosquito repellent

Ministry of Defence

Organisation that apparently consists of approximately 70 000 incompetents earning huge salaries and in line for massive pensions, which specialises in wasting vast quantities of taxpayers' money and serves no discernible useful purpose. Recent spectacular achievements (aka 'own goals') include almost giving away all our servicemen's accommodation to international financiers who have made gazillions from them; aircraft carriers that are apparently as much use as Mussolini's cardboard tanks; multi-role planes that are jacks-of-all-trades and masters-of-none, it seems; and destroyers whose propulsion systems simply don't work, or don't permit them to sail and shoot at the same time, which to this amateur at least seems a bit of a drawback.

Misplaced apostrophe's

(NB Do NOT write in complaining about this subhead: it's merely an unsubtle joke to make a point.) Look, I know this is hardly original, but it doesn't make the misuse of apostrophes an any less dreadful aspect of human behaviour, especially if you are particularly sensitive to grammatical improprieties of this type. Its occurrence is particularly offensive when it takes place in official communications, funded by the taxpayer who is about to be offended. An irony of the worst type, I think you will agree.

Missed opportunities for amusing 'twinning'

Britain has a marvellous collection of entertainingly named places — some of my favourites are Nasty, Loose and Milford Cum Lake (the mind boggles — especially when you realise that the sign is placed next to the village pond, which has a particularly murky aspect to it). So does France (Chez Bastard immediately comes to mind, but there are various versions incorporating Prats, for example, which are always good for a laugh). And body parts abound everywhere, including such gems as Peniscola, Labia, and our own Maidenpap, Fan y Big and Brown Willy. So why aren't the local authorities in these hilarious parts of the world doing more to optimise the opportunities for innocent lost-in-translation fun by more inventive twinning? I'd be happy to compile a database of candidates: submissions welcome. Your starter for ten — 'Pussy' on the road to the Trois Vallées.

Mobile phones

See Continually-being-reinvented mobile phone chargers

Mosquito repellent

Yes, you know the ones, don't you? Pale green with the feel of MDF. They look so cute, don't they, the two of them, so closely intertwined and curled up together in their packet for all the world like a pair of nesting baby vipers. To use them one at a time, as they must be, all you have to do is to separate the two green concentric circles of frighteningly fragile whatever. HAS ANYONE EVER MANAGED TO DO THIS WITHOUT BREAKING ONE OR BOTH OF THEM in the process, rendering them absolutely useless, because that curvy bit at the end, in the centre of the circle (you know, the bit that looks like a snake's head) has snapped off? And that's the crucial bit, because that's what enables it to sit in the little tin stand which supports the whole damnable contraption. At least Jeremiah Colman made his money from the fairly small proportion of mustard left unused on the side of the plate: the fiendish manufacturers presumably make their far bigger returns from the 90 per cent that's lying broken and unusable on the work surface, whilst the mosquitoes laugh at you.

And the sad thing is, next summer you'll go through the entire process all over again, labouring under the forlorn impression that last summer's incompetence was an aberration. No it wasn't, trust me. What you've gone through whilst being bitten to buggery by half the flying insect population of Provence is the norm. Head for the gin bottle to dull the

pain and the memory and more usefully to wash down the overdose of antihistamines which are your only real protection – and do what the Greeks do: burn a load of coffee grounds to keep the blighters at bay. On that note, obviously, one has to question the entire purpose of the mosquito. Why, pray, during the few days that Creation took, did God take precious time out to invent the mosquito? Or the moth, for that matter. And if he was so all-seeing, why did God permit the existence of the moth knowing that in a few short millennia the EU was going to ban camphor?

See also Midges

Motorhomes

Is it intentional irony on the part of motorhome manufacturers, do you suppose, that they brand their appalling products with such names as Swift and Rapide? Don't they KNOW that they will be driven at less than half the speed limit as likely or not by someone who looks like an escapee from an old people's home, as traffic jams miles long build up behind? And it's no good plastering them with go-faster stripes, zigzags and flashes of lightning that imply a potential for speed that will never be realised unless the brakes have gone and it's charging out of control down a one in five hill. Let's face it, they have the aerodynamics of a brick and drivers whose idea of fun is to enrage every other road user who's actually TRYING to get from A to B.

I'm prepared to make an exception for a proper Winnebago, with the length of an 18-wheeler, since they at least make no pretension to be anything other than a substantial home on wheels – and obviously those old-school VW campervans – but these sort-of-tuned-up transits with windows (complete with curtains, for Chrissake!) are a veritable plague and should be quarantined as such.

Movember

Once: laudable. More than once: merely tedious. Moustaches don't suit most people so please don't inflict your new look, however temporarily, on the rest of us. What looked impressive on a young Oliver Reed in *Women in Love* half a century ago isn't such a great look on a chinless under-manager today. Or his wife.

See also Dry January, Sober for October

Musty-smelling hotels

There's a unique odour to the third-rate hotels sector that should make you do a 180-degree turn and head for the exit the moment you encounter it as you step over the threshold of such an establishment. I've never been able to work out what it is, but the formula is likely to include aged carpet, poorly functioning vacuum cleaners, ancient breakfasts, travelling salesmen's socks, rough concierge's B.O. and other smells too vile to contemplate. It's unmistakeable and if bottled could surely take the place of all those exotic and far less lethal chemical weapons we read so much about, being off the list of banned substances and, one suspects, equally effective on the battlefield.

N

Name changes

What was wrong with Mesopotamia, Rhodesia, Constantinople, Mao Tse Tung (well, quite a lot in that case, as it happens), Bombay etc.? No prizes for guessing what the daily paper in Mumbai is called. And no – it's NOT the Mumbai Times. Funny, that. And Mao Zedong? Who gives?! And why can't I still travel to Persia? The same goes for pronunciation: whoever decreed, all those years ago, that Tutankhamen suddenly had to be Tutankhamooon?

And for pity's sake why can't I still lay out a few pence for a packet of Opal Fruits, when we all know that Starburst isn't a patch on the original, or chomp my way through a Marathon rather than face the embarrassment of asking the shop assistant for a Snickers? I mean – *a* Snickers? Didn't they teach ANY punctuation to the children who went on to become low-grade marketeers at Mars? Thank goodness one can still buy Parma Violets, though why a Derbyshire company came up with that name when it could so easily have been a good solid name like Bakewell or Buxton (oops, sorry, those names are already taken) defeats me. Here's a suggestion – Middleton-by-Youlgrave Violets: proper Derbyshire heritage, trips off the tongue nicely, and knocks Snickers into a cocked hat. And because of the length of the name, you'd have to have bigger packets, so you'd sell more. Think about it, Messrs Swizzels and Matlow: I promise not to charge commission on your future sales success.

Nannying

Yes, there's been a bit of rain. And the platform and the staircases might be marginally less grippy than usual, but do we REALLY need to be cautioned, over and over again, that this is the case, and that there is risk to life and limb from the extreme conditions we are experiencing. And who in their right mind would follow the similarly panic-stricken advice to 'hold onto the escalator handrail because of the weather conditions'? Everyone knows that that moving strip of rubber is home to billions of vile bugs that are way more likely to be injurious to your health than a misstep.

Do you EVER hear nonsense like this in Hong Kong, or Singapore, or Paris, for example? Nope. What IS it with public bodies in the UK that they feel the need to treat us as mewling infants at every juncture of our day?

There's way too much nannying going on, in all aspects of our lives…eating, drinking, smoking, recreational drugs, sport, walking, driving, gambling – you name it, someone is trying to get you to do less/none of it, do it more slowly/less frequently/more carefully/more thoughtfully! Go away – please – and let us make our own way in the world, if necessary enduring a few minor incidents along the way.

See also Health & safety, Hyper-parenting, Intrusive noise

Neck supports on planes

What is wrong with you?! Do you wear one at home, sitting on the sofa? Is your head about to fall off?! Aren't you already lugging enough superfluous items from place to place without adding a strange-shaped squidgy item that serves no obvious useful purpose. Bin it! You can't ALL have been on the wrong side of a tackle from Uini Atonio and are struggling to recuperate.

New loo rolls with the end stuck down

So – you've 'performed' – the loo paper has run out, and you go to use a new one. But you can't. Because the end has been stuck down with industrial-strength adhesive that can seemingly only be removed by the use of a blowtorch (which might render the whole exercise useless). So, already in some distress for reasons that don't need elaborating, you start to try to disengage the first segment of paper from its fellows. Of course, you already know what will happen: you will end up tearing various strips from not just the first piece but the next dozen or so, and wind up festooned with torn-off useless strips of paper, some metres long, before you get to the point where you reach a bit that's actually usable.

New Yorkers who loudly announce themselves and carry on talking at the tops of their voices

Look, I really like New York and have spent some very happy and productive times there over the years. I even like quite a lot of New Yorkers. But do they HAVE to talk so loudly and continuously about nothing at all? I remember once being in a restaurant in London, where a table of six New York women of a certain age didn't draw breath for a moment – with none of them giving pause to ever hear what any of the others were saying (to be fair, it was all pretty much drivel, as far as I could make out). That's all six of them talking at fever pitch simultaneously for the best part of an hour, in that distinctive twang. Enough to make one question the value of the 'special relationship'.

No dogs in pubs

Dogs have added to the ambience of pubs since time began, or even earlier. Maybe even all the way back to just after the Big Bang. So it stands to reason that pubs that bar dogs should be razed to the ground. And don't give me that, 'Oh it's an EU rule' nonsense: we all know that's as much a fantasy as the rules apparently insisting on straight bananas or square sausages. In France – part of the EU when I last looked – dogs are welcomed not just in bars but the finest restaurants, even to the extent of a chair being pulled up to the table for man's best friend to sit on, looking reproachfully at an owner who chooses a Badoit over a decent Burgundy.

See also No smoking in pubs

Noise (offensive)

See also Bagpipes, DJs, Estuary English, Fellow passengers, Hen parties, Intrusive noise, Jetskis, Loud mobile phonecalls, Loud/unamusing ringtones on mobile phones, New Yorkers, Piped music, Public transport announcements, Radio announcers, Shouty dads at school occasions, Simpering, Young people who can only communicate by shouting

No phone signal

How come I can download 100 Mb of a half-finished TV commercial on a boat in the middle of the Adriatic, recut it, and send it back over my phone, yet not get a decent enough signal in the middle of Soho to phone and book a table at the restaurant next door?! It's enough to make you emigrate. Just like when you buy a place in the sticks anywhere beyond the M25: before exchanging contracts you check if there's a half-decent signal. EE nope. Vodafone Yup. So you exchange contracts, switch service providers, move in, and within days your know-all neighbours are telling you that the Vodafone signal is invariably sh1t but the EE one is so strong you could use it to heat up your porridge. And it turns out they're right: what's all that about?! You sometimes suspect you'd do better with two empty cans and a length of string (thinking about it, that probably WOULD work with the restaurant next door).

No smoking in pubs

Can anyone explain to me why pubs were not left the freedom to decide whether they should be 'no smoking' or not? Or why they shouldn't have been allowed to retain a discreet area where smokers could do what they've done since Christopher Columbus almost certainly enjoyed his first swig of ale and a puff of his pipe in the Shit & Shovel half a millennium ago?

A by-product of this ban is that pubs now too often smell of vomit and wee – or, almost worse, those horrid little camphor balls that swill around in the urinal – where once they reeked comfortingly of cigarette smoke or weed (no pun intended). Or weirdly often, cooked fish, when this hasn't been served since a week last Sunday, when it was a 'menu special'. Maybe some public-spirited individual could invent an air-unfreshener that restores the smell of stale smoke that was once so welcoming.

And on that note, perhaps Messrs Dulux could bring out a paint colour to replicate that wonderful beigey-brown patina that white took on after a century of secondary smoking.

And whatever happened to pickled eggs, by the way? I could go on (and probably will).

See also No dogs in pubs, Scented candles

Not refilling ale glasses but starting afresh

Another one oft blamed on Trading Standards… 'ealth an' safety…the EU…management: 'sorry guv, not allowed to refill the same glass.' Why on earth not, for pity's sake?! I'm only going to recatch MY old germs, and I'm already pretty au fait with them. Just stick a second pint of Fursty Ferret in my endearingly smeary mug, pretty please.

And whilst I'm about it landlord, if I proffer my half-drunk pint and ask for a top-up, would you be so good as to do exactly that, and not make a show of producing a fresh half-pint glass, fill that, and expect me to consume from something so pathetically fey. It's just not manly.

Not washing after weeing, or worse

I remember once reading someone's reply to the question, 'Should a gentleman wash his hands before or after weeing?' This was along the lines of 'a true gentleman is highly likely to know what his todger has touched, even if his hands may been unwittingly soiled: therefore he should wash BEFOREHAND.' The sensible answer, of course, has to be both before AND after, in equal deference to the response given above and the realities of everyday life. I cannot be alone in shuddering every time I see a chap exit the loos without stopping to wash his hands before touching the door – and indeed everything else in the vicinity.

I've taken to carrying one of those small hygienic handwashes in order to minimise the possible effects of encountering the after-effects of such behaviour, as well as invariably pushing/pulling the furthermost parts of a public loo door to make my egress. This of course also underlines the grimness of the London Underground's exhortations to 'hold the handrail at all times': can there be any action more likely to spread germs?

All this puts me in mind of a long-serving cook at Ealing Studios, who I once witnessed in the bog, lifting his chef's uniform out of the way to reveal no underkecks at all, then using both hands to point Percy in roughly the right direction, perform, and then toddle straight back to his kitchen without a pause for even a minimal ablution. I never had much of an appetite on those shoot days.

On a similar note, but much more impressively, I was once in the next stall to Lord Hailsham in his dotage, who was by then pretty much disabled. It was entertaining to watch him prop first one, then a second walking stick under his bum like a shooting stick, so freeing his hands to do the necessary – before repeating the procedure to wash his hands afterwards. Breeding will out.

Officiousness

There's a particular category of uniformed behaviour that is simply intolerable: officiousness for the sake of it. To illustrate my point, I once was stopped on a commuter train coming into London, and asked to show my ticket and my railcard. For once, for some reason, I'd not got my railcard with me – but no matter, the ticket inspector confronting me was the very man normally on duty at my home station – whom I knew well enough – and who'd actually SOLD ME THAT RAILCARD not long previously. I pointed that out to him.

No problem, obviously.

B★LLOCKS!

I was fined £10 on the spot for not having a railcard. Cheers, MATE. Oh, and thanks for the tip that I could complain in writing to the rail company, explaining the error of my ways, enclosing all manner of evidence that helped prove my innocence, and I MIGHT get a refund of my fine.

Further up the carriage, a few moments later, my man came across a group of surly teenagers – all without tickets of any kind whatsoever.

Guess what? With a slightly despairing look – combined with a hint of fear – the inspector went on his way, nothing done. Inequitable doesn't begin to do this justice.

So here's a little rule regarding officiousness based on several decades of observation: if you are whiteish, middle-agedish, male(ish even), middle Englandish, the chances are you will be made an example of. You have been warned.

On the other hand, if you're a bat, or a toad, or a frog, or a newt, the official position will be to bend over backwards to care for your every need and satisfy your every whim. Think about it.

See also Officiousness

'On a journey'

Around the world in eighty days. The pretty much inevitable traffic jam between junctions 10 and 14 of the M25. The long-drawn-out development of a business plan that isn't complete sh1t. Only two of these activities could sensibly come under the heading of 'on a journey'. Your voyage to self-discovery, for example, is no more a journey than it is a voyage: it's merely an indulgence, love. And sorry, but your career path is no more a journey than a stretch of asphalt. Married life may, or may not, be strewn with roses, but it most certainly represents less a journey than a requirement for prolonged respectable behaviour.

What is it with this 'I'm on journey' malarkey? I think it's merely a posh-sounding phrase employed by people who actually have no idea where they're going, or indeed how to get there. So they dignify it with a pseudo-psycho kind of phrase to make them and their banal activities seem somehow more interesting. Ironically, of course, it has the exact opposite effect on most listeners. Normally, my immediate impulse on hearing it deployed is to embark on a journey to the nearest pub. Now THAT'S what I call a journey.

Onesies

Ugh. As attractive as a mankini, and only slightly more practical. Obviously useful to the parents of toddlers, but pretty despicable in all other circumstances. As an adult you CANNOT go around looking like an overgrown Telletubby and retain any self-respect, let alone the respect of others in your vicinity.

See also Sleepy suits

Openly displayed bakery products

Fresh bakery products good. But fresh bakery products in a display which encourages the depositing of every passing germ very definitely not. What's wrong with those little windows you have to lift open? And some tongs. Or better still, stack them behind the counter so a suitably protected shop assistant can reach them for you from a discreet distance. Simple concept: it's called a bakery shop.

Optics

What other civilised country festoons its drinking establishments with these devilish devices? Go to Spain, ask for a strong drink, and they'll keep pouring until a discreet nod of your head indicates it is time to stop. As a rough guide you should permit this activity to continue for a minimum of two minutes before commencing the 'nod'.

No one should need persuading that a 'pub measure' (enough gin, vodka etc. to barely moisten the bottom of a small glass) is absurdly small, and as such it is arguably the optic that has most to answer for. They should be removed without delay and humanely destroyed: in fact, a good case could be made for constructing special areas within recycling plants simply to permit the safe grinding down of these objects into their constituent parts and their reconstitution as something useful, such as hipflasks.

Option to tip offered when service charge already added

WHAT A CON! You approve the bill, which you note has already had an often unmerited 12.5 per cent service charge added to it – but which you're resigned to accept – and then when the waiter proffers you the card machine to approve the final amount you see that the first thing you are invited to do is to add ANOTHER gratuity. The cheek! Just NO. The previous 12.5 per cent has already taken the bill over your vague budget; the VAT the same again; to be prodded to add even more by way of a second tip could in all add over 50 per cent to the original charge. Taking into account typical restaurant margins, that could mean adding something like 90 per cent to the cost of what has been plonked in front of you. It would take a hell of a chef, sommelier and maître d' to make any experience THAT worthwhile.

Ostentatious physical exercises

Why can't people keep their 'PE' to the privacy of their home or the sanctity of the gym? Parading your pathetic scrunchies, jerks, planks, squats and so on in public is just – well, pathetic. I've seen people lunging at airports and even doing star jumps in the street. AND in Lycra. Gives a whole new meaning to the phrase physical jerks. And if you must warm up, please do so in your bedroom – not in the bus queue.

Out of season food

Time was, when we enjoyed runner beans, strawberries, asparagus etc. at the right time of year, which surely meant they were appreciated more. These days, however, we are regaled with all sorts of out of season produce the year round. Not only are they gobbling up the resources of the planet, but by and large they taste nothing like the thing they purport to be. Especially 'French' beans from sub-Saharan Africa for some reason, but broadly true of all fruit and veg that's travelled thousands of miles to sit, accusingly, on your plate, flaunting its carbon footprint at you in a very unappetising way.

Which begs the wider question of why so much produce travels so far. I had an acquaintance with a fishery business on Anglesey who told me that 90 per cent of the shellfish he caught was exported the next day to grace the tables of bistros in France, where unsuspecting British holidaymakers would be voraciously enjoying what they assumed was local fare. Why on earth don't they eat that kind of stuff back home? I can understand why tropical foods like bananas and guava perforce must make the long journey from field to fruit bowl – but the humble shrimp?

Over-engineering

Let's be clear. A boiler, for example, just needs to heat water and radiators and connect with a time clock and thermostat. And to do so without poisoning the household with carbon monoxide. Er, that's it. We don't want a fifty-page instruction booklet showing how all sorts of different means of varying the strength of the apparatus can be deployed – or a thousand permutations of time schedules be created. The same goes with watches: please just make it easy to tell the time.

And smartphones, eh?! Make a call? Tick? Send a text? Tick? Do emails? Tick? Take pictures? Yup. But please don't load it with so many absurd features that the battery barely lasts from breakfast to elevenses and that everyone sensible knows will never, ever be used, except by some Bill Gates-in-the-making nerd in the privacy of his own bedroom.

Over-packaging

So the courier hands you an enormous cardboard box, which you have no recollection of ordering, and you head indoors with the idea of opening it. You already know that you'll likely need a Stanley knife, scissors, maybe pliers/pincers, possibly a carving knife or tin snips…but even with your years of experience, are you braced for the barriers of materials which stand between you and your new acquisition? It is a fair bet that inside a carton measuring roughly nine cubic feet will be a small box whose dimensions are not much more than six by eight by four inches. This will be surrounded by layers of polystyrene whose forms would be the pride of Henry Moore or Barbara Hepworth; no doubt some of those strange inflated polythene squares looking for all the world like mini-airbags; possibly some wood shavings; maybe even some straw; definitely a lot more corrugated cardboard.

And then you get to the small object that on sight you now remember buying. As like as not, this will be hermetically sealed in rigid plastic and stuck to heavy-duty cardboard with the highest-strength industrial glue known to man. Tantalisingly, you can see your prize – BUT YOU CAN'T GET TO IT. Having sliced open your hand with the Stanley knife and spent twenty minutes doing that business with sticking plaster which is unusable if you only have the use of one hand, you are now INSIDE the pack. And then what?! It's damn well SCREWED to the backing cardboard with one of those Phillips devices. And what was the only tool you didn't think necessary for this complex operation?

That's right: a Phillips screwdriver.

It's enough to make you give up on shopping. For anything. For ever.

See also Chewing gum packets that disintegrate, Elastoplast

Overtaking on the inside

More commonly known as 'undertaking', a surprisingly prescient term given the likely outcome of the most aggressive form of this motoring activity. Normally very open to considered rule-breaking in the context of driving, this is one behaviour that I find unacceptable, especially since it is almost always exhibited by a spotty youth in a beat-up little car, both of which you KNOW will crumple in the face of any kind of a 'coming together'.

Overused/over-hyped descriptions

No, sorry, it's not AWESOME! It's merely alright. And it's unlikely to be AMAZING, either. Or FANTASTIC or WORLD-CLASS or any of the other PHENOMENALLY inappropriate superlatives in current-day usage. Our language is being drastically debased – oh, alright, slightly undermined – by the needless desire to big everything up. That climactic day at the 2012 Olympics when Brits seemed to win everything in sight was worthy of superlatives: merely contriving to carry two pints of beer and a bag of crisps from bar to table without mishap doesn't qualify for anything other than a small, discreet sigh of relief.

See also Wine descriptions

Oxford Street

London thoroughfare without a single redeeming feature aside from Selfridges. Full of other people, none of whom are looking where they are going; a great many very poor retail outlets; a large number of buses, all preventing the others from completing their journeys; and sellers of unwanted knick-knacks and souvenirs. Oh, and closing down sales that last for YEARS.

Oysters that refuse to open

After decades of dedicated practice, I'm a fairly accomplished shucker (never admit to this when six sheets to the wind, because of potential mispronunciation issues), but every so often I will come across an oyster that resolutely refuses to submit to the knife. Here's some sensible advice: simply set your ego and the oyster to one side and move on to the next one. If you don't, you'll only be defeated and likely end up with a livid cut in the fleshy part of your hand that will take weeks to heal. It's said that more than 2000 Frenchmen are admitted to hospital annually on New Year's Day having suffered such a wound, and the accompanying nasty bacterial infection that often results. You don't want that.

But what is with uncooperative shellfish in general: a whelk whose contents refuse to emerge however much wiggling you do with a cocktail stick; the winkle in which nothing whatsoever turns out to be residing, after ten minutes of poking about; and the prawn that squirts that nasty orangey gloop all over your freshly laundered white linen shirt as you twist it in half just as lunch on the first day of your holiday is getting underway? And as for langoustines – lots of early promise but eventually precious little to show for your efforts. You work away at it for what seems an age, enduring a couple of nasty nicks in the process, and eight inches of natural packaging eventually gives way to produce a minute quantity of unedifying white stuff. But back to langoustines...

P

Pampering

Where/when/why did this vile phenomenon first appear? The gym/spa manager who first came up with the proposition that pampering should be part-and-parcel of some girly awayday should be assigned to a year of intensive re-education at a brutish bootcamp in the Falklands, and be informed in advance that it was a great new concept entitled Mollycoddling for Men, and he was a very lucky boy to have won a place on the course. So lucky, in fact, that he would be the only person on it. Ever.

See also Simpering

Paris

Once lovely, now sadly somewhat seedy, city in western Europe. One used to put up with the snobbery, anti-Englishness and lack of civility there because so much else was good. To make the City of Light seem slightly more desirable by comparison, loiter for a while at Charles de Gaulle airport or worse, the Gare du Nord: from then on, everything will seem *merveilleux*.

See also South Kensington

Passport control

If you've ever flown into Bordeaux, you'll know where I'm going with this. Behind their frosted glass window they wait – dozens of them: customs officers – to be sure the BA plane that's been timetabled for well over a year has landed, and then they hide in their back office. Once the queue has built to a nice round hundred or so, one of them saunters out, fires up his computer, removes various items of clothing, showily readjusts the seat he was sitting in five minutes earlier, and starts to look like something is about to happen.

Of course, the computer won't work first time, and even though the official has scanned tens of thousands of passports in his time, he behaves as if this is the first time he's bent one backwards and slid it into the little scanner in front of him. Tricky stuff. But eventually he accomplishes it, comes to the realisation that you're not on a mission to kill the entire population of Aquitaine – and lets you through, grudgingly.

Meantime, now that the queue has built to something like a hundred and fifty people, all desperate to get into Bordeaux's city centre for an already late supper, a second official ponderously makes his way from the back of the two-way mirror behind which he's been sniggering, and starts the same process himself. It's GOT to be a traditional Bordelais game – but then it happens in Vegas, and Dubai, and – yes – even Gatwick, so maybe there's a WhatsApp group called something like 'bordercontrolbastards' on which they share 'intel' and inspiration.

And it works both ways – by which I mean, trying to leave Bordeaux. If there are two of you together, let one of you try to proffer your boarding card AND your passport: I guarantee that the boarding card will be impatiently thrust back at you. The second of you should then just hand over the passport, at which point, with a grim inevitability, you will be asked to show your boarding card as well.

See also Officiousness

Patronising policemen

'It's at times like this that accidents happen,' said the absurdly young, but obviously and oxymoronically worldly-wise policeman to me, when I'd left the car briefly to make a phone call before the days of mobile phones. It was pouring with rain… we were moving house…we'd arranged for my wife to return to tow the 'wouldn't start' second car to the new address…but I managed to get it going and needed to tell her. Big mistake: I'd left the engine running whilst the car was unattended. Criminal behaviour, obviously, in respect of an ancient, battered, Fiat Panda that no self-respecting car thief would have gone within a mile of. Three points, thank you very much, Mr Patronising Policeman.

See also Policemen pretending to be helpful, Sarcastic policemen

People who confuse the concepts of 'working' and 'being at work'

Hardly surprising, really, I suppose, after decades of schooling where just turning up from time to time was enough of an achievement for a worryingly large proportion of the population. And I'm not just talking about builders who spent much of their working day leaning against the side of their Transit puffing on a rollie and perusing the pages of *The Sun*, before heading off for their third full English of the day, or the legions of FBers, Tweeters and IGers who believe that a significant part of their daily duties consists in keeping *au fait* with their status on social meeja.

I think I may be talking about the vast majority of the working population, with the obvious exception of anyone happening to be reading this IN THEIR SPARE TIME. Only this can explain why – whatever I've said elsewhere – per capita GDP in the UK is lower than France, of all places.

Evidence is all around you, and de facto, the noisier the 'worker', the less effectual he/she/it is likely to be: I give you the bossy aircrew who stamp up and down in cheap high-heeled shoes, achieving nothing but rising levels of irritation amongst their passengers; restaurant table-clearers who try to outdo each other in their crockery clattering and only serve to annoy; and – worst of all – busy-busy keyboard typists, who apparently were only put on this planet to test various mechanisms for elevating blood pressure.

People who don't watch where they're going when they're looking at their mobile phone

Ouch! How many times have you involuntarily collided with someone obsessing over the latest bikini pics on their Instagram feed or updating an expectant world on their Facebook 'status'? There's even an acronym for them: SMOMBIES (smartphone zombies, since you were about to ask).

Why can't you sit down and complete these vital tasks before recommencing your walk? Must you multi-task in such a needless fashion, putting others at risk of serious injury? Have you NEVER heard of risk assessments? Hmm, that's obviously b*llocks. Whatever, just stop it.

People who engage in longwinded conversations at check-ins

Why? What is there conceivably worthwhile to talk about? Go away.

People who get into an Underground carriage before those on board alight

What IS it with you people?! Is the concept THAT hard to grasp?! There's no point whatsoever in shoving your way into an already crowded tube carriage only to find that you're now impeding the egress of passengers only too keen to make space for you. It's not merely an etiquette consideration – it's pure common sense. Which of course precludes the majority of the population and almost all visitors from overseas, it seems, from abiding by such a simple rule of life.

People who get to the front of the checkout queue then find to their astonishment that they have to pay for what they've put into their trolley

Let's face it, it's unlikely to be the first time they've ever gone shopping, so the experience of a transaction involving the exchange of money for goods won't be an entirely alien one. But you'd think it was an utterly bizarre and new-fangled practice, judging by the number of times the queue behind them is held up by the simple request from the checkout girl for some form of payment for the tonnage of items they've spent fifteen minutes bagging. 'Oh, money? You want PAYMENT?!' you can almost hear them thinking. 'Extraordinary! Well, let's see what I can do to satisfy you.' There will then as like as not ensue a frantic scrabbling and searching for a purse... notes...coins...credit cards...anything that might do. And then – horror of horrors (though you knew it was coming and were about to mime the words) – the checkout girl asks, 'Do you have a loyalty card?' This will almost certainly induce a blinding moment of excited panic (think St Paul on the Road to Damascus and you're not far off). You then know you're in for another interminable session of bag-searching before the loyalty card is unearthed. Joy! Your turn next. But you know what'll happen now, just like at an airport check-in counter: they'll want to CHAT...

See also People who engage in longwinded conversations at check-ins

People who pretend not to realise that there is a queue

You know the type...you've been queueing for well over half an hour, obviously loathing it (but in a fatalistic kind of way), when someone does a sort of soft-shoe shuffle, sideways-ish, face averted in fake unawareness, and – wow, how did THAT happen? – ends up immediately in front of you. This could be at check-in, passport control, waiting for the loo, a bus stop...no matter where, there's a chancer who has convinced themselves that they are somehow elevated above us mere mortals and for whom queuing is therefore an affront to their natural superiority.

There then arises the obvious question – how best to let them know that their sense of superiority is ill-founded, and that hell has a special place reserved for people like them… where there is NO QUEUE WHATSOEVER. They'd be in like Flynn, you can assure them. In fact, you'd like to say, the gatekeeper will beckon you forwards the moment you're spied, lurking – with no sense of irony whatsoever – at the very back of the queue which leads to the nethermost sulphurous pit.

But back in the real world, and no doubt aware of the risk of being stabbed with a machete, you resort to fixing their back with a steely glare and muttering in a stage whisper all sorts of disparaging comments – wasted on them, you realise too late, on account of their massive noise-reducing earphones, which they no doubt forgot to remove last night when they finished their shift as a ship welder. Probably.

Personnel

The correct word – normally used in conjunction with the word 'department' – to describe the branch of a sub-industry now inexplicably with an independent life all its own and known by the impressionable as 'human resources'. Parasitic in nature and essentially non-productive, the 'personnel department' more than anything serves as a backstop for dealing with the outcomes of awkward, badly thought-through management decisions. A backwater best paddled clear of by people of talent. The vogue phrase 'Talent Acquisition' is clearly meant ironically, since the last thing anyone working in a department with a nomenclature like that will be capable of is spotting anyone with anything approaching talent.

Pesky pool inflatables

It was OK when the most you'd be expected to blow up was a small rubber ring or a pair of armbands, but in this era of giant lobsters, flamingos and unicorns, you can spend half your holiday inflating all manner of objects which, once up, maintain your offspring's interest for all of ten minutes, leaving you – ears popping and eyes bulging – gasping for air for the rest of the morning. And what is it with these new-fangled valves that you have to squeeze whilst blowing, or that have that annoying little flange inside that never comes free, so all you do is experience a dramatic blow-back which gives you a lasting face-ache? And why are those foot-pumps they sell you so utterly useless? Has ANYONE been able to use one without getting serious leg cramp – always assuming that the last person to use it hasn't mislaid the one nozzle that's the right size for the 20ft diameter blow-up pizza you're about to get to work on?

Pet shops with appalling names

What IS it with pet shop owners that, like tattoo parlours and hairdressers, they have to demean their trade with such ghastly puns and poor stabs at creativity? I mean… 'Paws 'n claws'…'Squeaks 'n Squawks'…'Petcetera'…'Heads to Tails'…and the omnipresent (it seems)…'Pets in the City'. For God's sake, there are even WEBSITES dedicated to helping the hapless wannabe pet shop owner pick an appalling name. Kindly spare us the lame names and stick to something workmanlike that doesn't make you want to drown your kittens – something like 'The Pet Shop' should do it.

See also Hairdressing salon names that try to be amusing but aren't, Puns

Photocopiers that devour paper and refuse to disgorge it

In other words, ALL photocopiers. You know what happens: an orange warning light starts flashing the moment you have the temerity to press START, and those precious papers you'd spent an age preparing for a meeting that's due to start imminently disappear into the maws of a machine whose innards probably still contain chewed-up images of your secretary's arse from two Christmas parties ago. It starts to spell out unintelligible instructions, which inevitably consist of pushing, pulling or prodding a whole series of differently coloured levers. These of course have no effect whatsoever, but you will occasionally get a glimpse of snarled strips of heavily inked bits of your document, looking for all the world like the detritus left the morning after a drunken game of Consequences. My advice? Ring Personnel and leave a message (they won't be there) and blame someone else when you have to act out your presentation like a game of Charades – as if it was always meant to be that way.

Photographs of food outside eating establishments

It is a truism that every restaurant/bar/café that displays pictures of meals on its exterior – or indeed in the pages of a naff menu – with the intention of making one's mouth water is certain to achieve the opposite effect. Can anything be less likely to boost one's appetite than a badly photographed plate of food, badly cooked and badly arranged? Well yes, actually. When just such photographs have been hanging around for years and have mellowed with age, so that everything is a pale, seedy yellowy-beige hue and curled at the edges (a bit like the photos of houses for sale in rural French estate agents). Why do they do it? Do they ever look at the fruits of their labours and wonder why, as soon any self-respecting prospective customer sees it, they turn on their heel?

See also All-purpose oriental restaurants

Piercings

For generations, male gypsies were known to wear a gold ring in one ear to pay for the cost of their funeral. This is a very rare instance of a practical purpose to a piercing. All other manifestations of piercings in the male are to be abhorred, and indeed the majority of those in the female. Do your ears REALLY need to be festooned with a bewildering variety of adornments, or a hole drilled through your earlobe, like those primitive natives in some far-flung jungle that used to be the stock-in-trade of *National Geographic* magazine? And does your tummy button, front bottom, mouth, nose, cheek or even breastbone need to have a hole drilled in it so that you can dangle something of dubious aesthetic value from it? I think the test is simple: if you're a girl and have a piercing in the lobe of each ear for a tasteful earring, fine. If you're anything other than that, or are fiddling with a different part of your anatomy, then very much not fine. I hope that's clear.

See also Tattoos

Piped music

Why?! OK, so some piece of amateurish consumer research once suggested it put people more in a buying mood. For anyone normal, it simply puts you in a vile mood. Or worse. Many years ago I spent several days shooting some pedestrian commercials in what euphemistically was termed a 'furnishing centre'. In reality, it was a very big shop that sold very horrid furniture. Be that as it may, any prospect of calm was destroyed by the continuous sound from a STRETCHED audiotape, that repeated itself hourly from 9 a.m. to 6 p.m. How I wish we'd been engaged in a synch-sound production! No such luck.

At the end of day three I asked one of the shop assistants if the muzac didn't drive him mad. At that moment, as I looked at him, waiting for his reply, I realised that he'd been driven clinically insane many years previously and had in effect become lobotomised. He drifted away, aimlessly, half-heartedly humming a tuneless melody as he went.

That excellent organisation Pipedown should immediately be awarded a Royal Warrant and the right to issue plaques commending establishments that refuse to deploy intrusive never-ending compilations of easy-listenin', soul-destroyin' muzac. Offenders, on the other hand, should be made to sit through hour after hour of uninterrupted Harrison Birtwistle interspersed with anything by Wings – WITHOUT comfort breaks. I swear they'll get the message...

See also Atonal music

Piss-taking cab drivers

Before Uber – and before TomTom, Googlemaps and all the rest – it was black cab and Addison Lee drivers who boosted their takings by taking you on a completely unnecessary circuitous route to your destination. And if you knew the roads better than them and had the temerity to assert – however tremulously – that this might just be the case, you were almost certain to receive a barrage of abuse, possibly extending to threats to dump you on the back streets of Willesden at dead of night, and consequently at serious risk to life and limb. That behavioural streak has now of course been inherited by a legion of Uber-driving Bulgarians, whose knowledge of the capital is likely as extensive as their grasp of post neo-classical endogenous growth theory.

The b*gger of that, of course, is that these days you can SEE the evidence for this on your smartphone, as you watch your intended chauffeur slowly wend his way in your direction before suddenly veering off in the complete opposite direction. Guys – it may SEEM like this, but the City ISN'T actually a maze, created intentionally to entertain car drivers through bafflement and thereby treble the length of every journey: don't you HAVE one-way streets in Sofia? I know you have cul-de-sacs, because I've checked on Google Translate – just don't go down one, ever, puhlease.

But, of course, this phenomenon isn't confined to London. If, like me, you happen to know New York, Rome or Paris, for example, really quite well from years of close acquaintance, it is galling to find a cabbie assume that you're in total ignorance of the local geography and are fully expecting the trip, say from JFK to Downtown, to take in the sights of Yonkers and so bring the bill to way over $100. London-based foreign-seeming people have told me the same thing applies here, and invariably return home after their UK posting overly familiar with the back streets of Willesden, even when home was a rented house in Battersea. 'Sarf of the river, guv? You mean across the sea?! Sorry, you must be joking…never go there.'

Poetry that isn't

Anyone with a basic mastery of English can string a few lines together that are essentially gobbledegook and that don't rhyme, but please don't kid me that this is poetry. The late much-lamented Mr Palgrave, he of *Golden Treasury* fame, would be turning in his grave at some of the stuff masquerading as poetry that gets published by such people as recent Poets Laureate.

REAL masters of the art are the creators of such rhyming gems as 'Turd right' for 'Pirbright', 'truncheon' for 'junction', and 'whistle first' for 'Chislehurst'. You will no doubt have your own favourites. Here is a simple test that is perfectly safe to try at home: to judge whether a work is poetic a foolproof method is to look at the end of each line and ask yourself…Does it rhyme with the last word at most a couple of lines above or below? Painless. Bring back Mary Wilson, that's what I say.

Pointless sports

Curling. Speed skating. Nordic Skiing. Egg & Spoon races. League Two division football. Archery for the Blind. That velodrome event where everyone on a bike manically chases a small moped faster and faster till they all fall over. All absolutely fatuous, obviously. Inventive and eminently watchable activities like Extreme Ironing and Topless Darts, on the other hand, are rare and honourable exceptions to the extensive list of sports in which there is no point whatsoever. But, synchronised swimming…dressage…WWF…the Highland Games – if it looks kinky, it probably is, and should be prohibited for the sake of public morality.

Policemen

See Policemen pretending to be helpful, Patronising policemen, Sarcastic policemen

Policemen pretending to be helpful

'You can go that way if you so choose, but I cannot recommend it' is the kind of thing they must teach in level one at the Hendon Police College. It's the sort of thing third-rate schoolteachers would say to a surly fourth-former. A sort of 'take it from me, sonny, I know best'. Not if you're a wet-behind-the-years recent recruit to what I believe is referred to as 'the job', you don't. 'Move along there now, nothing to see here' is another one: wrong – OF COURSE there's something to see here, OFFICER, that's why we're all craning our necks to get a better view. Show some common sense, dammit!

Talking of which, on the subject of most policemen's – or is it now policepeople's? – abject uselessness, it may be worth recounting the events of an early Sunday evening in sunny Hertfordshire. We had a short gap in the schedule to take an overseas visitor to St Albans. Halfway down the slip road to the M1, we found that the motorway was locked solid with traffic, which we simply did not have time to enjoy on this occasion. So along with many others, we put our hazard warning lights on and gingerly reversed a hundred yards or so back up to the roundabout in order to take a different route. Immediately we all encountered a gleeful pair of motorway cops who were in the throes of getting their month's quota of convictions in one fell swoop by doing the lot of us for dangerous driving.

Appearing in court some weeks later, on being asked if I had anything to say, I replied that since we were paying for the police 'service', mightn't it have been more in the nature of a 'service' for the police to have been stationed just BEFORE the slip road rather than after, inviting drivers to enjoy the traffic jam if they wanted, but if they had other priorities, giving it a miss might be a better idea. Good point, said the Chairman of the Bench, halving my fine and thanking me for my inventive suggestion. I have every confidence this is now in Level 2 of the Hendon Police College course – an object lesson in sensible twenty-first-century policing.

See also Patronising Policemen, Sarcastic policemen

Politically correct

Ah. Now we come to the nub of much that is wrong in Western society. I'm going to be un-PC (not for the first time in this tome, as the more diligent amongst my readers may have noticed) and say that I really can't be arsed to enumerate the manifold ways in which the practice of ensuring political correctness is destroying the very fabric of civilisation. I'd very much like to say something like, let's call a spade a spade and have no truck with PC-ness, but that would no doubt be disallowed for fear of offending the over-sensitive. Am I permitted therefore to assert that we should call a spade a f*cking shovel, or will that risk upsetting shovels that can't f*ck. Where will it end?! The temptation to sit – man-spreading all the while – in a public bar, cradling a whisky and puffing at a cigarette whilst perusing porn on the iPad, and maybe occasionally inviting someone passing to 'cop a look at the top shelf on that', before breaking wind in dramatic fashion is sometimes almost overwhelming. Tell me I'm not alone.

See also Positive vetting/stereotyping

Positive vetting/stereotyping

How likely is it REALLY that the elderly lady with the double-barrelled name from the Home Counties leaning heavily on a William-Morris-patterned walking stick and carrying a copy of the *Daily Telegraph* is trying to sneak on board the components of a bomb in her Cath Kidston carry-on bag? Is it really necessary having partly stripped her in front of dozens of fellow travellers to brusquely march her off to a side room for 'special measures'? Have some common sense and a sense of proportion for God's sake! The most offence she is likely to cause is by sucking a Werther's Original audibly with her dentures, and that's easily dealt with by confiscating them because they contain liquid. More likely wannabe terrorists are unlikely to carry Werther's Originals because of the risk of discovery: THEY should be the ones treated with suspicion.

Obvious, really, when you think about it.

See also Airport security, Politically correct

Potholes

With the bulk of our money spent on fatuous stuff way outside their original remit (support groups, propaganda, pay-offs and the like), local authorities no longer have the means to repair the potholes that bedevil our roads, damaging thousands of cars weekly and putting cyclists' lives at risk. Have they never heard the valuable saying, a stitch in time saves nine? In this case, a timely dollop of tarmac that could prevent the development of a pothole big enough to swallow a double-decker bus a year hence.

PowerPoint

The scourge of modern day commercial life. Makes one almost hanker after the days of the overhead projector...or before then, the 35mm slide show...or the Nobo flipchart (in the latter's case even because of its capacity for inflicting maximum and hilarious embarrassment on the next person to use the damn thing, because someone's drawn something extremely crude eight pages down from the top sheet and – schoolboy error – you forgot to check). Simply encourages those with zero capacity for original thought to indulge themselves with the notion that quantity is better than quality, especially when it's got SO MANY COLOURS and GRAPHIC DEVICES and SHOUTOUTS and CHANGES OF FONT.

Here's a simple test. Print out that PPT presentation in black type on regular white paper. Suddenly you'll realise how completely facile it is, and that all that cod creativity is merely a camouflage for its essential vacuity.

Predictive text

N9pkkoxkd! That's the sort of helpful word that's likely to appear in your message if you try to type in the word 'b★llocks', something I find myself doing with remarkable frequency as it happens. Odd, that. How dare my phone try to second guess what I'm about to say – and THEN GET IT WRONG! It's not just presumptuous, it's offensive. Just as when my phone tries to sign me off as Jenry. What do those techy chaps in Seoul or Silicon Valley know of the English vernacular, for pity's sake? Maybe there are lots of Jenrys in their neck of the woods – but even so, they very definitely deserve a kick in the n9pkkoxkd. And while I'm at it, Mr Apple-mac man, I'LL be the one who decides whether I want a capital letter at the start of my email address or not – nOT You. See waht I meen?

Premature promotions

Listen here, Mr Selfridge, the Christmas season does NOT start with the return of children to school for the Michaelmas term. The start of Advent is quite soon enough to festoon your shop with Christmas paraphernalia. And in the same way, Mr Cadbury, kindly restrict the sale and promotion of creme eggs to the couple of weeks immediately before Easter, not the minute that Epiphany has run its course. Mothering Sunday, likewise, does not need months of revving up, any more than the price of flowers need revving up the day before. Father's Day, as we all know, is merely a marketing contrivance to compensate for the seasonal downturn in Hallmark's sales and so should receive no publicity whatsoever. Whereas St George's Day…? Don't get me started.

See also Back to School, Prolonged poppy-wearing

Pretend working class

We all met them at university. Boys (it always seemed to be boys) who after their gap year suddenly mislaid their privileged Harrow/Winchester/Shrewsbury etc. background and affected a worker's mien. And like all converts (non-smokers, arriviste Roman Catholics), not just holier than thou but with a zeal about them which was nausea-inducing. Look chaps, you're not the ragged-trousered philanthropists reincarnated; you're just posh gits trying to sound like yobbos. Get over it – that, and your recently acquired averred preference for Newcastle Brown Ale over Beck's – in time for the recruitment round for the magic-circle lawyers.

See also Estuary English

Prolonged poppy-wearing

In the naturally ordained order of things, poppies should be worn in the immediate hours preceding, during or immediately after the eleventh hour of the eleventh day of the eleventh month. In other words, during Remembrance Day. The only acceptable additional occasion is the Sunday closest to it. To wear a poppy on any other occasion is to commit the gravest faux pas, so all that prominent 'virtue-signalling' in the weeks beforehand is deeply, irredeemably naff. Almost as bad is the continued display – sometimes for years – of a large, faded plastic poppy hanging skew-wiff from the radiator grille of a battered Skoda.

See also Red Nose Day, Virtue-signalling

Pub barmen who are crap at their job

'Pint of bitter, please.' Fatal request to a useless barman whose command of English is limited to a grunted "'Ello' and who's probably teetotal him/herself. Ugh. Holding back the urge to jump across the bar, wrestle him/her to the ground, and grab the beer pump yourself, you wonder how much of your expensively obtained pub-based education to impart. So you meekly tap the fount, mouth the word 'pint', and gesture with your hands the charade that hopefully communicates 'a large one', before watching him/her incompetently overfill a glass with foam that you know will take the best part of half an hour to subside and the remainder will be pretty much undrinkable. Pour it down the SIDE of the glass, for pity's sake!

See also Incompetent cocktail barmen

Public displays of affection (PDA)

Public displays of affection are obviously to be deplored, especially when it's the kind of smooching that involves a lot of audible slurping or visible exchange of bodily fluids. I'm not even sure about hand-holding by anyone beyond their mid-twenties. American Presidents and their wives do that, and it's almost certainly axiomatic that more ardent the PDA in later years, the less genuine it is. Think David Mellor at his farm gate with his long-suffering wife in the wake of the unfortunate adultery episode, for example.

What the tabloids tend to refer to as 'full sex' (yep, I know it sounds gross) in public can be more entertaining and somehow less tacky. As well as a dodgy Amsterdam restaurant where couples would copulate in fishermen's netting above the heads of the diners, I remember a young couple making out, their movements easily discernible, under a groundsheet right in front of us at a crowded open air summer concert in Kenwood. To the strains of the closing movement of the '1812 Overture' as I recall, climaxing with a splendidly apposite fireworks display. We should definitely come again, we chortled, loudly enough to be heard (we hoped).

Public transport announcements

'See it. Say it. Sorted'. That's one of the latest manifestations of this malaise. I've actually had to vacate a train carriage for some gulps of fresh air whilst the recorded announcer got this latest glib bit of nonsense off her chest. And at the time of writing, it plays at every station stop – the discomforting effect emphasised by its simultaneous appearance as a moving, backlit series of words where only station names should appear.

And what on earth is the point in stating over the PA system, 'Bicycles are not permitted on this station unless they are already folded' if you've just turned up with your £8000 carbon-fibre roadbike. Bit late, eh? How were you to know?

And why the newish warning about being careful not to drop your mobile phone BECAUSE IT MIGHT FALL DOWN THE GAP BETWEEN THE TRAIN AND THE PLATFORM EDGE? So might you, Mrs Nanny Announcer, if you don't shut up!

But then I hanker after the long-off days of the live announcer who every evening welcomed me home with the words – memorably recollected by Clive James – 'Kembrardge,

Kembrardge. This is Kembrardge…' Received pronunciation at its very best – the effect only slightly marred by the fact that you were almost always forty minutes late and had been stuck a short walk away waiting for the platform to clear for half that time. Happy days.

Then why, alone of all underground networks anywhere in the world it seems, are we constantly adjured in London 'not to run on the escalators…hold onto the handrail…' etc.? Every ten seconds! Don't these people know that it was a rite of passage for every self-respecting schoolboy to run UP the longest DOWN escalator he could find (top prize was Angel)?

And why in so many other British locations are we continually warned that, 'We are approaching the end of the escalator: START WALKING NOW'? Are these particularly difficult escalators, egress from which is only effected by very delicate manoeuvres perfected after months of dedicated practice, as if one were heading for the Winter Olympics Ski Jump? No, it'll be that some busybody has decided to try and secure extra plaudits from Health & Safety for the absurd over-provision of safety-related announcements. Ye gods!

And has the direct inverse correlation between the frequency of public transport announcements and the utter lack of necessity for them ever been the subject of an academic study? Or to put it in plain English – why is there a plethora of fatuous announcements over the PA system when there is NOTHING WHATSOEVER THAT NEEDS SAYING and complete radio silence when there is a crying need for information? If you've ever been stuck on a train in total darkness for an hour without explanation, or at an airport where all the flight notifications have disappeared and no queues are moving you'll know exactly what I mean. Nothing…not a peep…total radio silence…complete absence of uniformed attendants: you can't ALL be on a refresher course about optimising microphone management.

See also Health & Safety, Nannying, 'There's a good service on all Underground lines', Warning labels

Pubs

See also Fake candles, No dogs in pubs, No smoking in pubs, Not refilling ale glasses but starting afresh, Optics

Puns

Only rarely acceptable, clever or amusing. Too many are simply cringeworthy. Most likely to be acceptable only when spontaneous/unrehearsed. Invariably bad news when contained in newspaper headlines, whether advertising or editorial – the more contrived, the worse, naturally. Frank Muir's description of a smoking concert as 'a soirée with a binge on top' is up there with the best. 'The wurst is yet to come', announced by one incredibly inventive customer to an impatient one in a Berlin restaurant is the only recorded joke in the German language.

See also Hairdressing salon names that try to be amusing but aren't, Pet shops with appalling names

Pushy parents

If you've ever made a commercial or been involved in an amateur dramatics production that requires the presence of children, you will have encountered that uniquely unattractive phenomenon: the pushy parent. No, little Johnny isn't destined for the next lead role in *Billy Elliot*: he can't take direction that requires him to take just two small steps and smile, looking directly forwards. You've been trying to get him to do that since 9.30 a.m. and it's now 3.30 p.m. and the rules require that his limo takes him home. Immediately. So you're looking at an extra shoot day at a cost of something like £50K thanks to his utter uselessness, and his parents are asking how soon you could help him get an audition in the West End. Look, you want to say, he can't walk, he can't smile − as far as you can see his talent merely extends to pulling faces at the other children, snivelling and asking to be taken to the bog, and for that he's being paid £300. But instead you sidestep the question, point him in the direction of the Grip who will enjoy the extra attention (Mum's not bad-looking) and who's heading outside for a fag, and retire to the relative safety of the production office. 'Never work with children or animals', as the cliché (sorry) has it: dead right.

See also Hyper-parenting, Shouty dads at school sports occasions

Q

Quasi-famous 'lifestyle' bloggers

Vloggers etc., arntcha sick of 'em?! Instagram influencers, brand ambassadors, lifestyle coaches, mentors, you name it – they all belong to the same category of over-weaning self-regarding fatuity. And yet the buggers make money from it. Footballers get to drive flash cars, for no discernibly obvious reason. Princess Eugenie's husband gets rewarded for promoting an obscure brand of tequila. Pretty girls seem to swan around the world in a succession of bikinis at other people's expense (nothing wrong with that, you might say, with reason, that's the way it's always been since the first cave-dweller's fancy piece strung a few bits of antelope hide together to make an alluring two-piece). Self-appointed parenting gurus called things like 'mummy with the mostest' hand out moth-eaten homilies like a medieval travelling preacher. And so, nauseatingly, on.

I think a little more honesty/realism in lifestyle blogging would make the whole practice more acceptable. After all, not everyone gets to jet all over the place in little more than a £500 pair of crystal-encrusted knickers and a pout. For example, I once got more than 120 likes on Instagram to a photo I posted of the departures board at Waterloo on a rainy Tuesday evening plastered with 'CANCELLED' notices. And not a pair of bikini bottoms in sight (I did check, obviously). Why not Gatwick Airport's North Terminal on the first day of the school summer holidays? Or a lane closure on the M1? Or an image of fog or drizzle or Margate (or all three in one – hardly difficult to accomplish, naturally)? You might not earn anything much from such activities but at least you'll enjoy the warm glow of having contributed to the general wellbeing of mankind.

Questionable children's names

So a couple of thousand years or so of human history hasn't given you choice enough? I mean Kyrie, for God's sake?! And Zak. And Trixiebell. And Dwane, Shane and Wayne. And children named after the places in which they were conceived, though I'd make a special exception for 'Bikeshed', as in 'Let me introduce you to my good friend Bikeshed Brown.' And then the parents have the nerve to refer to these as Christian names! I don't think so. I remember some years ago talking to the retired headmistress of a grammar school about their selection process, thinking naively that it would all be about the children's marks from primary school…their personal statement, etc. etc. Not a bit of it, she replied, more than half-seriously: we go through the names of the applicants and know intuitively, based on years of experience, which forenames almost certainly denote the kind of pupil we absolutely do not want to darken our door. A simple but self-evidently effective screening process – and one founded on an obvious truth (but one that dare not speak its name).

I name this child Phuket Beach... Sorry how do You pronounce that?!

R

Radio announcers

What IS it about this trade? The moment they enter a studio, sit on that swivel chair and adjust their microphone for height and distance, they invariably take on a whole new persona. What's that about? Do you simper in real life? Is that how you got the job? Do you laugh at yourself ordinarily – or continue to chuckle at unfunny things the moment you leave the studio? Deadpan delivery would be better for my money. Or just dead. Pirate radio was never like that, nor the Third Programme: why Classic FM, Heart and all the rest – including now, sadly, Radio 3?

See also Simpering

Raising the pitch of your voice towards the end of a sentence as if asking a question when you're actually making a statement

Can a whole generation's speech patterns REALLY have been affected by the way that actors in such series as *Neighbours* and *Home and Away* deliver their lines? Or is the snowflake generation so unsure of what they're saying that they tend to frame pretty much everything as a query rather than a definitive comment? Tiresome – that's the word for it. More antisocial than Antipodean.

Rawlplugs

See also half-in/half-out Rawlplugs

Ready meals

Renowned for their over-reliance on the use of a microwave not to mention salt, sugar, taste-enhancers, stabilisers, preservatives, colouring, over-packaging, fake-gastro names and misleading food photography ('Serving suggestion' – yeah, right, be honest. It's a CON – you know it, we know it). Clearly, there's nothing wrong with such ready-to-eat staples as proper pies, sausage rolls or Cornish pasties but pretty much everything else in the category is over-contrived and to be avoided if you wish to die at a reasonably advanced age.

Reality TV

Apart from news programmes, all that most civilised TV viewers (I know, something of oxymoron, sorry) want is a mild form of ESCAPISM from reality, not to have a particularly vile version of it rammed down their throats of an otherwise inoffensive evening. Why are the people/places/participants/presenters/ programmes all SO IRREDEEMABLY GHASTLY? Why are they all fake-tanned to the max, as like as not under-dressed, and seeming to lack a single positive personality trait? Who started it? I blame that Bazalgette fellow (scion of the sewer-inventing family – funny that!) for creating *Big Brother*. Whatever, please can we have a reality-check, not a referendum obviously, because that's sure to go the wrong way – culled from a few carefully recruited focus groups maybe, and destroy this phenomenon before it destroys civilisation itself?

See also Any TV or radio show with audience participation

Red Nose Day

Would you believe it's as long ago as 1988 that the first Red Nose Day was held? Nothing wrong with that: a 'good thing', as the authors of *1066 and All That* would doubtless have averred. But does it have to come around with such monotonous, charitable-spirit-exhausting regularity? And as for that faded red nose still stuck on the front of an ageing Volvo eight months after the event, please – it's still a Volvo and nothing will make it sexier.

See also Prolonged poppy-wearing

Red ropes outside wannabe in-demand venues

It is axiomatic that the less in demand a venue is, the more substantial the red ropes outside restricting entry. In fact, there's probably a direct inverse correlation to be drawn between the undesirability of a venue and the extent of red 'ropage' outside. And don't you hate the flourish with which a third-rate doorman lifts the rope aside when someone whose name is on the list arrives?

Reloading the dishwasher
for no good reason

It would be hard to think of a more extreme example of the weirdness of human behaviour than the fetish exhibited by someone completely rearranging the dirty contents of the dishwasher when another willing party has already – thoughtfully, and with all due consideration – loaded it. Does it REALLY matter if the cups are where you'd rather have the mugs, or the bowls where you want to put the plates, or that the spoons have been mixed up with the forks? It's not a question of aesthetics for Chrissake! It's simply a machine: you place mucky things in it, in a reasonably logical order; put that funny little tablet in its little compartment; close the door; press the button; and retreat to a safe distance. Take it from me: NO ONE WILL EVER KNOW WHAT IT LOOKS LIKE INSIDE. And when divorce looms with near-inevitability, please don't tell me that this is one of the grounds you'll be giving as unreasonable behaviour: GET OVER IT!

Reply to all

One of the most lethal aspects of the computer age. How many careers and private lives have been wrecked by the careless misuse of this button? Back in the day, you'd have had to print off multiple copies of whatever document you were preparing, sign them all individually, and physically post them off. How likely was it, under that regime, that your boss would have received a communication from you stating in no uncertain terms that you think he is a w*nker of the first order? Or that your best friend would discover that he is not quite so best as he thought he was?

The answer is simple: internet service providers should immediately withdraw this facility and require users to physically add names to the distribution list, so virtually eliminating the opportunity for embarrassment or worse.

See also Email strings

Restaurants that can't cook as well as I can

I'm well aware that I'm no Heston Blumenthal (though I've been known to swear like Gordon Ramsay), but I seriously resent it when a relatively pricey restaurant turns out to be incapable of cooking or presenting food as well as I can. Medium-rare steak that's hard and blackish on the outside and cold in the middle? Hake that's dry, flaky and falls apart the moment you touch it, a bit like the roast turkey in *National Lampoon's Christmas Vacation* but less amusing?

Overcooked prawns with the texture of plasticine? Cold salad on a warm plate? Hot food on a cold one? You get the picture – oh, and while I'm on about it, at the end of it all a minute, bitter espresso in a cup that's four sizes too big and has clearly been kept in a deep-freeze for a year. Rant over.

Restrooms

No they're not. They're lavatories.

See also 'Where's the bathroom?'

Revolving doors that are way more complicated than they need to be

I remember once reading that revolving doors were introduced as a means both of maintaining a reasonably constant temperature in a building and minimising the effects of air pressure, wind etc. Fair enough. But why do they sometimes have to be so damn complicated?! Am I alone in finding it near impossible to detect in advance whether it's one of those which sets rock-solid and refuses to budge the moment you touch it, or one that will be rock-solid until you touch it?

And what's with those ones with built-in segments like triangular shop windows that use up valuable space and simply serve to irritate, with their naff displays of plastic plants trying to kid you about the building's green credentials? Very odd.

Ridiculously closely targeted advertising

Just because I once inadvertently stumbled upon a website promoting young ladies' underthings doesn't mean I wish to be pestered with ads for all kinds of risqué lingerie and related racy items till my dying day. So Mr Google, please take your algorithms and stick 'em where the sun don't shine. I am, after all, after a lot of inappropriate practice, perfectly capable of tracking down a web merchant who is in the business of selling saucy knickers all on my own, in the unlikely event that I want to, I just don't wish for my dodgy peccadillos/healthy interests to be thrown back in my face every time I switch on my computer. Or worse, when someone else does...

Room fresheners

What's wrong with opening a window? And if you really want the smell of an alpine forest go for a walk in one. What really did it for me was the sight of a Royal Warrant in the lobby of a multinational HQ which read, 'By Appointment to HM The Queen Mother, the makers of Magic Mushroom'. I can just imagine her nibbling on hallucinogenic fungi, washed down with copious amounts of G&T – but a plug-in air freshener?! Hmm.

See also Scented candles

Rubber mats in playgrounds

Grazed and bloodied elbows and knees are surely vital rites of growing up: deprive our children of the right to incur modest self-inflicted harm and who knows what will happen further down the line. No doubt some ridiculous risk assessor started the trend towards 'safe play', but it's a safe bet he/she was a desk-bound wimp whose idea of a childish adventure was more likely to be playing doctors and nurses than pooh sticks. William Brown will be turning in his grave – and maybe even Violet Elizabeth Bott too.

See also Hyper parenting

Rucksacks

Acceptable whilst hillwalking but not otherwise – especially on the Tube. Why do people NEVER realise how much they stick

out, and persist in hitting you when they turn around? Even the Hunchback of Notre Dame would have had a better sense of self than today's space invaders all geared up for a day at the office in a way that wouldn't disgrace someone about to attempt K2 in the depths of winter.

Rules

'Rules are there to be broken' – or at least undermined by a modest amount of piss-taking. I have a theory that if there were more fatuous little rules that those inclined to a little gentle anarchy could enjoy breaking, then the more important ones (like quiet zones in train carriages) which keep society civilised would stay mostly intact. In other words, people could satisfy their innate desire to be rebellious and so make a little statement about their independence without doing any actual harm.

At school in the fifth form, it was the compulsory wearing of ties and caps that produced marvels of ingenuity, staying just within the school rules in the spirit but not to the letter, with a tie that was half an inch short or three feet long, for example, or a cap that was so re-engineered that it sat right on the back of one's head in an ironic fashion that simply underlined its sheer fatuity both as a rule and a garment. For me these days, for example, the pleasure of taking a short cut at Embankment station from the Circle/District Line down the No Entry stairs to the Northern/Bakerloo lines is a happy combination of the knowledge that you're saving yourself at least forty-five seconds whilst at the same time cocking a snook at authority. Try it – you'll get a real buzz, I assure you. It's the same dizzying emotion as one gets from crossing a road ANYWHERE BUT a zebra crossing, just to save maybe fifteen seconds and get a little adrenalin rush, both from the naughtiness of it and the slight sense of danger (but not in Singapore, where you'll up in jail).

Rustling

This is not about the endearing sound of a baby hedgehog snuggling down in a pile of leaves. On the contrary, this is about one of the nastier forms of human behaviour.

Whoever invented those plastic bags that aren't soft but somehow crinkly? Were they DEAF?! And why do the possessors of such infernal devices persist in continually shaping and reshaping them, opening and close them, and rearranging the contents the entire length of the Tube journey from Cockfosters to Piccadilly Circus?! And for some reason, it was decided that the inner packaging of breakfast cereals should be constructed from the same damnable material. For use at BREAKFAST TIME, of all hallowed hours!

It's just the same with crisp packets. All you should need to do is simply pull it open with a single deft movement that takes a split-second. You can then insert your fingers and neatly remove the requisite number of potato crisps. There is ABSOLUTELY NO NEED WHATSOEVER to fiddle with the wretched thing interminably, as if the only way you truly appreciate the value of your purchase is by maximising the sound effects.

Plus, of course, there's the unintended (one hopes) side effect that, just as with stage whispers, ensures that the harder someone tries to muffle the sound, the more intrusive it becomes. A slowly unwrapped sweet held under the programme notes on your lap in an otherwise silent theatre? A packet of ibuprofen capsules under the table during a brain-numbing meeting? Christmas presents under the tree on Christmas Eve? I rest my case.

s

Safe spaces

If you're sojourning in Syria, for example, I can see the merits of having a safe space to which one can retreat to avoid the undoubted ghastliness that surrounds you. But on a university campus? If you wish to escape the attentions of the gender police, or chuggers, or campaigners, or people with bad hairstyles or unfortunate clothing, then surely all one needs to do is to take oneself off to the kind of space people like that are unlikely to invade. A branch of John Lewis, for instance, or a field, or the library.

See also Snowflakes

Sagging trousers on youths

Yes, they've been around a long time, and we've all heard the notion about their origins (hand-me-downs from big bro's in poor families: yawn), but that doesn't make them acceptable. They still look as though they've followed through in their kecks, and are about to lose them. More than faintly ridiculous, obviously, though probably best not to point this out.

St Patrick's Day

By and large, the only obvious signs that it is St George's Day are flags flapping gently from the top of a few church towers. But for St Paddy even the waterways in places like Chicago are turned green in celebration. The world over there is a riot of Gaelic lettering, fake shamrocks, leprechauns and Guinnessswilling. What has made it quite so infectious and – well – naff? I'm almost inclined to have a pint of the black stuff every other day of the year BUT St Patrick's out of sheer cussedness.

See also Too-frequent fireworks displays

Sales

Doesn't everyone know that these are mostly utterly fake? Just so long as an organisation abides by the law, with for example a jumper priced at, say, £7000 for half an afternoon in a remote, seldom-visited branch of a clothing store, then a subsequent sale announcing 3000 per cent off can be held. Almost all the stuff you see in shops at sale time has mostly been bought in just for the purpose of creating the means to announce a sale. All that Last Day, Must End Soon, Special Purchase, Black Friday, Bank Holiday Special, First Day etc. etc. malarkey really should be seen for the nonsense it is. I mean – have you ever actually seen any smoke-spoilt items in a Fire Damage Sale, or shrunken ones in a Water Damage Sale? Thought not. So next time you see a poster advertising a sale, do bear in mind that if something looks too good to be true, be assured – it almost certainly IS.

Sales conferences

A day – or maybe more – set aside by a business when a load of pushy sales-types can flaunt their dubious successes, and their less successful colleagues be amusingly humiliated, all in the cause of learning from best practice or some such corporate b*llocks. Significant quantities of low-grade alcohol is likely to be used to lubricate this hateful event – and in the old days, a bus-full of low-grade ladies especially hired in to massage egos and more – together with a plethora of PowerPoint presentations, flipcharts, wipe-boards, pointers, 'break-out groups' (God help us), and the inevitable D-grade chap from off the telly to regale us with his exciting inside tales of life in 'the meeja', and as like as not entertain us with his ability to get all the names/attributes wrong of the people he's been briefed to poke fun at, all the time thinking he's God's gift to this proletarian gathering. Is it conceivable that any sales conference has EVER actually achieved anything beyond mass hangovers and a dispiriting sense of life's innate futility and a determination to change jobs as fast as possible?

See also Consultants, Middle managers

Sarcastic policemen

'What does that round red sign with a white bar across it mean?' asked the supercilious copper early one morning in Marylebone – the same one who a few minutes before had written down my surname in his notebook with two Ts rather than one, and, when I corrected him, averred, 'I'm feeling generous today.' Sarcastic sod.

Do you suppose there's a module in police-people's training courses entitled 'How to sound helpful to the general populace but at the same time have the inner joy of secret sneering'? That would explain why another plod years before asked me in a tone that might have been coached, 'Would Sir care to walk his bicycle home rather than ride it, given that it has no lights or brakes, the tyres need inflating, and Sir is somewhat the worse for wear?' To be fair, I had just none-too-gently come to a halt in his crotch, owing to the absence of lights, brakes, decent tyres and a superfluity of Adnams.

See also Patronising policemen, Policemen pretending to be helpful

Saturday night TV

Have you ever met ANYONE who has watched television on a Saturday evening, unless it's to catch up with something previously transmitted? Am I the only person in the UK to be allergic to the inanities of game shows, talent shows and the like? And am I the only football follower who has to leave the room to avoid the music for *Match of the Day*? Whoever schedules this sort of rubbish is without question the kind of person who is always either down the pub for the evening, at the opera, or attending a dinner party on a Saturday whereby he/she knows there is no danger of catching any of this sordid programming: there is no other explanation.

See also Daytime TV

Sausages

We were once all perfectly content with proper British bangers, containing a bit of meat together with a lot of other more suspect ingredients. Surely nobody ever wolfed down a few of those in the belief that they were paying homage to the body-as-a-temple? So what is it with these absurd deviant varieties shoved chock-full with things like onions, herbs, vegetables and other culinary peculiarities *de nos jours*. And while I'm at it, a word on appearance. All you have to do is – whether under the grill or in the frying pan – keep turning them, so that the entire surface area is satisfactorily browned, and not just a miserable percentage of it. That way you are pretty much assured of a sausage that is as enjoyable as it is aesthetically pleasing.

Let us have none of that off-putting, insipid pinky-beigeness so beloved of low-grade hotels, where they've probably been broiled for a moment by a kitchen worker who hasn't the genes of generations of British-breakfast-sausage-servers, and then fleetingly shown a hot surface in a vain attempt to mimic proper sausageness.

Scented candles

Candles good. Scented candles bad. Simples. And as for those ghastly scented room fresheners/plug-in devices that squirt probably lethal chemicals into the air – how did humankind survive for millennia without them? Do you imagine that cavemen or the aspiring middle classes of the Middle Ages, for example, sat around thinking, gosh, wouldn't it be marvellous if someone could invent an apparatus that would alter the chemical balance of the air we breathe and try to kid us were savouring the aromas of a forest in springtime? Never mind the wheel or the flushing water closet, what we really ache for is a synthetic smell.

See also Pampering, Room fresheners

Scottish football news

Why? Who wants to know? Where are these places anyway?! It's enough having to sit through the Vauxhall Conference League or similar without having results from some faraway place of which you've never heard inflicted on you. And aren't they mostly always postponed thanks to bad weather, anyway?

Scrambled eggs

Why do so many people – professional as well as amateur cooks – find it SO DIFFICULT to dish up scrambled eggs as they should be? That is to say, not rubbery, not cold, not flakey, not runny, not lumpy, no colour other than a glorious sunny yellow hue, no black bits from the bottom of the pan. And DEFINITELY never, ever from a packet. You half expect inedible scrambled eggs from a low-rent hotel backing onto a provincial airport, but I've had to turn down eggs with some or all of these faults in some of the world's finest hotels.

Listen up – it's simple: with a fork, whisk up the requisite number of eggs with a dash of milk or cream, and some freshly ground salt and pepper. This takes maybe thirty seconds. Heat a decent dollop of butter in a pan and swish it round, before pouring your egg mixture into it. Turn it over/break it up with a wooden spoon fairly frequently for a few minutes. Then serve, not whilst it's in the least bit runny but before it gets rubbery. If you want to be fancy, sprinkle a few bits of parsley or chive over it, and then garnish with properly cooked, good quality bacon and sausages, black pudding, tomatoes, maybe some mushrooms, but never, of course, baked beans. Likewise, tomato ketchup should never be used to anoint your scrambled eggs, since this is off-putting for fellow breakfasters on account of its faintly murderous appearance, for all the world like the leftovers from the St Valentine's Day Massacre.

See also Boiled eggs, Sausages

Screw caps on wine bottles

Or even worse – crown caps. Yes, yes – I know that up to 10 per cent of all natural cork stoppers are somehow infected with a bug (hence most cases of bottle-stink or corking), but I remain convinced that there are few things more distasteful than the contents of a fairly promising bottle being kept at bay by a screw cap. Kindly restrict their use to fizzy drinks, and let wine-lovers risk the occasional duff bottle through the aesthetic enjoyment of cork.

Selfies

By all means, take a picture of, for example, Big Ben whilst you're there, if you must, but puhlease... don't stick your own goofy face in front of it. I'm pretty sure I'm on safe ground in asserting that was NOT what Sir Giles Gilbert Scott had in mind when he designed it.

And as for selfie sticks – we keep thinking they're dying out (a sure sign of this is when they're given out in 'goodie bags', free at conferences and exhibitions), but then another A320 full of Far Eastern trippers arrive and they're all over the place again. Absurd.

Sellotape

Has there ever been an invention more calculated to drive one to distraction than Sellotape? More specifically, has there ever been a habit more damnable than not bothering to turn the end over after use, so that the next comer is doomed to spend half an hour trying to identify where to start? How CAN it be so invisible?! After a few minutes of using your fingernail and being bewitched by false clues (a ripple in the Sellotape doesn't necessarily indicate the end, you will have noticed), there is nothing else for it: you take the sharpest knife you can find and with the confidence of a neurosurgeon cutting into a scalp, attack the roll at right angles. What happens next is utterly predictable: a long strip of quadruple-thickness tape unravels, consuming about a quarter of what is left, and then just as you at last reach the bit of that to attain normal thinness, it splits and sits firmly back on the reel, leaving you exactly back where you started, but this time festooned with an unusable length of tape to dispose of.

I don't think struggling to open your sellotape roll warrants a call to Samaritans Rob

And please don't tell me to get one of those poncey little plastic Sellotape dispensers. Not only will you look like a try-hard office assistant in a sitcom set in a 1950s typing pool, but IT WON'T WORK. The tape will keep coming adrift from the little teeth that are supposed to hold it in place, and you'll be staring at the same problem as described above. Sadly, there is NO ANSWER.

Shouty dads at school sports occasions

It's SCHOOL sports, gentlemen…not a grudge match between Wimbledon and the MK Dons. We just don't want to listen to your exhortations to little Edgar on the merits of tackling 'ard. And nor on a gentle summer's day do we want the sound of ball on willow to be disturbed by shouts of 'That was LBW, you w*nker!' If you MUST behave like that, take yourself and your urges to Australia, where apparently they like that kind of thing. Maybe little Edgar could get a sledging scholarship…

See also Pushy parents

Shovel action by people eating

Behaviour out of which people should grow by the age of, say, three. Unless you're from the New World, it seems, in which case it is de rigueur, or you've just bought a takeaway bowl of cheesey beans from the old-school caff at Guildford Station, in which case understandably you have little choice (but you can at least stand with your back to everyone to eat, lest you offend someone of a sensitive disposition).

See also 'Holds knife like pen'

Showers that are impossible to work

There was a time, and I promise you not merely glimpsed through the most roseate-tinted spectacles imaginable, when if you wanted to have a shower in your hotel room or the house you'd rented, all you had to do was step into the shower, turn the mixer tap to your preferred temperature, and there you were – a SHOWER! No longer. Nowadays you are likely to be confronted with a bewildering array of controls that wouldn't have been out of place on the footplate of the *Mallard*. None of them, of course, will have any obvious function, so you will find yourself experimenting increasingly desperately for half an hour when you could have been enjoying a fatboy's breakfast. During the course of this you will likely have blasted your genitals with a jet of cold water that comes at you horizontally at precisely the level no one sane could want, painfully reminding you of nothing less than standing exposed at the foot of the Reichenbach Falls on a February morning. And not in a good way.

I need hardly add that ALL these controls are at the far end of the 'wet room', meaning that you have continually to reach through the torrent of water coming at you from all angles and at all temperatures just to have half a chance of any kind of a shower. All very well for the S&M brigade but for anyone whose idea of a reasonable shower is a gentle introduction to the day ahead, anything but.

See also Taps/plugs that don't work

Simpering

Am I alone in ranking simpering close to pampering in the nausea-inducing stakes? Both should clearly be outlawed – and by that I don't just mean the words in all their ghastliness, but the actions they suggest. Double jeopardy obviously applies to someone who simpers whilst pampering (a regrettably frequent occurrence), or vice-versa. A 'pampee' subjected to both these extremely disagreeable experiences should without hesitation do a runner, possible lack of clothing notwithstanding.

See also Pampering, Radio announcers

Sleeping policemen

An artificial obstacle placed in your path which makes driving anywhere increasingly fraught. Mankind has spent thousands of years trying to get from A to B more quickly: in the last few decades the powers-that-be (who ARE they?) have invested heavily in achieving the opposite effect. For pity's sake – why?!

The average speed of a journey on wheels through London is apparently now less than it was a century ago. Once-straight roads are often now meandering obstacle courses, with all sorts of street furniture and plantings stopping anyone from getting anywhere in a reasonable time. The only time I managed to raise a smile when confronted by a series of traffic-calming measures, was seeing a sign announcing 'Humps for 150 yards', under which some obviously randy teenager had scrawled, 'Yes please!' (Almost on a par with 'St

Matthew's Close', under which some wag had written, 'Well, I can't see him!')

And is it me, or do traffic lights nowadays work far too slowly – strangely, apart from on the occasions when YOU are the pedestrian and then they seem to take for ever to change in your favour.

See also traffic calming measures

Sleepy suits

A rather pathetic air steward once asked me at the start of a transatlantic flight, in that special cloying voice they tend to deploy, 'Would sir like a sleepy suit?' The temptation to say yes and then smother him with it was almost overwhelming. Instead I asked for a whisky, which of course couldn't be served until we were well airborne and the 'fasten your seatbelts' sign was extinguished. Maybe whisky is lethal below a certain altitude and sleepy suits aren't…but I cannot see the logic in this, having enjoyed whisky at sea level on more than one occasion.

Sleet

Wearisome halfway house between rain and snow. Snow has its purposes (e.g. snowmen, skiing, tobogganing, snowballs, getting a day off school), as does rain. Sleet self-evidently serves no useful purpose whatsoever and is just misery-inducing, especially when it gets under your shirt collar.

See also Drizzle, Slush

Slush

Greyish, unsatisfactory material left to fester when snow starts to melt. Deeply unattractive – cannot disappear fast enough – screws up your train service – destroys your Gucci loafers – and does nothing to contribute to the gaiety of life. Unlike snow, which brings joy to the young-at-heart and the necessary conditions for skiing.

See also Drizzle, Sleet

Snowflakes

Indispensable in a snowstorm, but thoroughly useless as members of the human race. I recall reading that the police were finding it difficult to cope with these overly-sensitive creatures as recruits because, among other things, they don't like confrontation. Bit of a basic qualification for someone whose entire career will be founded on telling other people what to do/not do, I'd have thought. 'Hello mate, my machine is trying to tell me that you were breaking the speed limit, but I can't believe that's right. Is there something you'd like to share with me?' On reflection, as a chronically badly behaved motorist, a cohort of snowflake speed cops might be just what I've been hoping for in the past half-century…

So

So. 'My car wouldn't start, so I phoned the RAC'. THAT is one of the correct usages of the word 'so'. Though I bet you just left the lights on all night long so the battery drained, SO you're almost certainly at fault: WHATEVER.

Properly, the word 'so' might be an adverb, a pronoun, a conjunctive, an interjection ('So! I see you have discovered my little secret, Mr Bond' etc. etc.) or even – though I'm not really sure about this – an adjective most often heard in third-rate musicals ('Tell me it ain't so, honeybunch!'). But one thing it really can't be is the time-buying (shades of Harold Wilson taking an age to light his pipe, before saying, 'I'm glad you asked me that, Robin.'), slightly hesitant, inappropriately drawn out intro to a response. When did all that start, eh? By whom? Timing-wise, I'm guessing the start of the twenty-first century. As to usage, I really cannot improve on the information provided by the Urban Dictionary: 'the first word of any answer given by a know-it-all douchebag. . .in order to feign superiority.' Love it.

So – there you have it.

Sober for October

Apart from the obvious hideousness of the concept of being sober for an entire month, isn't it blindingly obvious that Sober October has only come into being as a PR ploy entirely based on the oh-so-clever rhyme.

And as for Dry January, it hasn't even got a rhyming scheme to commend it. That month is already bloody enough, what with getting over Christmas and New Year, braving the winter, and facing the prospect of a massive credit card bill at the end of it. If do-gooders MUST have their alcohol and not drink it, then I offer up 'Parched March' as a compromise through which to exercise their overworked social consciences AND satisfy their need for poetical expression.

But please – count me out.

See also Dry January, Movember

Sourdough bread

You SURE about this? Sure it's not another case of the emperor's new clothes? It's neither fish nor fowl – well, obviously it's not – but setting that aside, is it actually NICE? Is everyone pretending to like it because they daren't risk losing face by owning up to finding it a bit, well, tasteless, and with the consistency of mdf (that's medium-density fibreboard in case you're wondering)? Look, I'm not saying we have to revert to the days of Sunblest and the not-so-great British sliced white, but we're not ALL allergic to all things once considered utterly normal, so an occasional piece of proper thick white not-overdone toast is hardly too much to ask (although it obviously is anywhere remotely woke, like Hoxton).

See also Woke

South Kensington

Trying desperately to seem like a 'quartier' of Paris, and in large part succeeding thanks to the attitudes of many of the arrivistes, who have brought with them their often unlovely Gallic attitudes, incomprehension of the concept of queuing, perpetually moody teenage daughters, etc.

See also Paris

Split infinitives

Better-known writers have banged endlessly on about this to no avail. Would you all kindly please just stop it. Maybe the rot set definitively in with *Star Trek* and its badly worded mission statement (actually, aren't they all?). Now look what you've gone and made me do…

Sponsorship 'bumpers' at the end of a commercial break

That's right. You've NEVER seen a good one. They're all sick-makingly awful, even allowing for the restrictions on what you can do/say in the few seconds you have. No, Mr Director, you're not creating the next *Ben Hur*, just a few seconds' promotion of some undistinguished new car from a brand no one's ever heard of and is unlikely to buy. Please, please don't pretend to us – or yourself – that it contains a storyline and is going to be worth watching: just GET IT OVER WITH! And while you're at it – elbow those clichés and puns (verbal, visual or both): you're in the way of my programme.

See also Clichés

Stag weekends

At bottom, everyone knows it should be a Stag NIGHT not a weekend. The kind of thing that was good enough for me (five pints of Wethereds Bitter and a bag of smoky bacon crisps in The Gate at Bryant's Bottom, since you ask – most famous for its length of tilted guttering pressed into service as a urinal) should surely be good enough for all.

See also Hen Parties

Station Stop

No it's not. It's a station. Or a stop. As in 'the next station is…' It's not both: please don't use twenty words when one will do.

See also 'We will shortly be landing into…'

Sticky labels that refuse to unstick

How many times have you bought a paperback with a sticker on the cover advertising its brilliance or cheapness, and found that it is impossible to peel off? You start to work your thumbnail under the edge, only to dislodge a bit of the first layer of the sticker, which leaves you with that objectionable underneath layer part-revealed, and which you know in your heart of hearts is stuck fast for infinity. This means that you will forever be looking at a part-removed sticker which announces that the paperback you eventually half-read was apparently brilliant/cheap, but which you only remember for its promotional sticker's intransigence.

Alternatively, you set to with a kitchen spatula and lighter fluid, gradually progressing to a wallpaper scraper and white spirit, which inevitably leads to a small heap of gluey scraps of paper part-dislodged from the book cover and a never-to-be-dislodged stain where the sticker once was. Over time, because a faintly sticky residue will inevitably remain (the glue they use clearly has a half-life on a par with the disused nuclear rods embalmed for eternity at Sellafield), your book cover will gradually attract a collage of household dust, mites, cat fur etc., so that eventually it becomes for all the world like one of those touchy-feely books beloved of nursery schools.

The same is true in equal measure to bouquets of flowers (have you EVER succeeded in scraping a sticker off a cellophane florist's wrapper?), wine bottles and the box of chocolates that you bought as a present but which inappropriately shouts BUY ONE GET ONE FREE in huge letters, and is sure to diminish your stature in the eyes of the intended recipient.

See also Glue that sticks to everything but what you want it to, Over-packaging

Strategy

Nowadays an absurdly overused word in all sorts of inappropriate contexts. Strategy is what military commanders like Napoleon, Wellington, Clausewitz, Rommel and Monty did, with varying degrees of success, not junior marketing people or 'consultants'. Provincial marketing communications agencies hope that by bolting this word onto their list of offerings, they sound more serious. Ironically, it has the opposite effect.

See also Consultants, Middle managers

T

Tans

See also Bad tans

Taps/plugs that don't work

Why, oh why are people continually reinventing the tap? The Romans had them. They were perfectly serviceable generations ago. And yet hardly a week goes by without one being confronted with a diabolical new contraption that has none of the intuitive tap-like qualities that would render it the slightest bit fit for purpose. You encounter taps with no discernible moving parts; taps that turn in precisely the opposite way you would expect; taps that produce a small waterfall for all the world like an element in a Japanese garden; and worst of all, taps that supposedly react to hand movements without being touched at all. These of course invariably produce no water whatsoever, and you flap your hands around ever more dramatically in the hope of getting SOMETHING to happen, before giving up completely. To compound your humiliation, the next visitor to the hand-basin that you've spent ten minutes trying vainly to activate has to only look like he might be mildly interested in a spot of ablution for the tap to gush forth like Old Faithful. Bizarre.

And what about plugs in hand-basins and baths? Time was, when this was a simple circular object, as like as not made from black rubber, and held in place by a small chain. To use it, you simply put it in place – and hey presto, there it was! Hole plugged (the clue is in the name). And to remove, you simply yanked it free with the chain – the work of a nano-second.

Hah! Far too obvious. We've now caught the French disease of plugs that require a number of different components (levers, screws, rods, handles etc.), mostly hidden so out of sight and reach that when something goes wrong you might as well take a sledgehammer to the sink and order a new one, as try to get the wretched thing to work after it's gone on strike.

But we, of course, have gone one better. Not content merely with aping the French, we've introduced a whole series of new variations on a theme: more levers; more rods; more screws; plugs that swivel; plugs that supposedly work by suction (they never do); and plugs in theory coupled with some device far-removed from the plughole but that refuses to do your bidding.

You may not have known of its existence, but you already know the gist of Becket's First Law of Hotel Bathing Culture, which states, 'the posher the hotel, the more likely that the contraption designed to prevent the egress of water down the plughole will defy every reasonable attempt to use it'. Which, of course, means that you regretfully end up trying to have a shower, when Becket's Second Law of Hotel Bathing Culture kicks in: *see* Showers that are impossible to work

See also Too many other entries to be worth listing

Tattoos

Acceptable in seamen and some ex-servicemen, if sufficiently orthodox in design and not too gaudy. Otherwise, very ill advised unless discrete and aesthetically pleasing, which on the evidence pretty much everywhere, is unlikely. Don't you sometimes wonder what all these extensive and increasingly ubiquitous installations of body art are going to look like when the owner is in their eighties? Will the photogenic Cheryl's expanse of roses still look in the least attractive half a century hence, when it's pretty gruesome to start with?

One of the few examples that actually made me smile, was a navel surrounded by a circular design stating 'Made in England'. Almost all others, unless they are a Chinese symbol that the owner thought read, 'Oh magnificent One' but actually translates as 'I am a self-satisfied, ill-educated, misguided tosser', are to be deplored. Was there ever a more apt bit of slang than tramp-stamp?

See also Piercings

Tautology

I was tempted to write 'whoever first coined…' in an earlier entry, but happily noticed my near faux pas just in time. Tautology isn't merely inappropriate wordage, it is also self-evidently time-wasting and as such to be avoided in order not to commit a grave social solecism. Oops, there's another.

Team-building

An activity sponsored by organisations, both commercial and not-for-profit, that almost invariably has the precise opposite effect of what is intended. You will forever hold in even more contempt than you started with, the person who took seriously the challenge of crossing a stream with two pieces of corrugated cardboard, a length of hosepipe, four bulldog clips and a dog lead. And then had the nerve to look pleased with themselves when they accomplished it. Team-building activities almost always end up with several colleagues coming to blows in the bar afterwards, and at least one unwanted pregnancy. To be steered clear of at all costs: throw an inventive sickie – you'll gain their respect by your ingenuity if not from your prowess at overcoming fatuous challenges.

See also Consultants, Middle managers, Sales conferences

Teapots/kettles/jugs that refuse to pour accurately

Wouldn't you have thought that since the primary – or at the very least, secondary – function of a teapot, kettle or jug is to be able to pour from such a vessel without spilling half the contents, that the designer would make at least a cursory effort to ensure that this is possible. But no – many such people obviously take a perverse, not to say wicked, pleasure in knowing that from the day it is cast until the day the damn thing breaks it will NEVER pour in the way one might reasonably expect. Pouring contraptions have been around for millennia, so one could be forgiven for thinking that the design challenges of a pouring lip that actually delivers the goods would be a problem that has been long since cracked – probably about the same time as man discovered how to make fire, and perfected by the 'beaker folk' some 4000 years ago. But, no. Maybe this is a challenge that Mr Dyson of vacuum cleaner fame might like to rise to.

See also Taps/plugs that don't work

The easily offended

'Look away now'. 'Some people may find what follows offensive'. 'Contains moderate scenes of sex and violence'. 'Some swearing'. Look, if you're so ridiculously sensitive, why don't you retreat to the safety of your room, snuggle up in a onesie with a Peppa Pig compilation and don't reappear until you've grown some. And definitely don't buy this book.

See also Snowflakes

The fashion industry

An oxymoron, obviously, with the emphasis on the last two syllables. It's dressmaking, or millinery, or sewing. Whatever, it's most definitely not an industry. A trade which employs chalk-faced, anorexic, eggy-looking girls barely out of puberty to promote its wares surely cannot be dignified by the word 'industry', with its respectable overtones of hard work and heavy machinery. No, let's call it out for what it is – a somewhat suspect, deeply meaningless process by which every half-year or so most of the female population are persuaded to part company with a great deal of money for a number of small items of clothing bearing a very close resemblance to the ones ('so last year') that they've just dropped off at the charity shop.

The M1

An unrelievedly ugly road, featuring semi-continuous roadworks, that joins the south of England with the Midlands, and as such is therefore a bad thing in its own right. When you also consider that it is largely jammed with unhappy people in slow-moving vehicles driving north or south in a forlorn attempt to sell things to each other, its sheer pointlessness becomes apparent.

The National Anthem

This is no reflection at all on Her Maj, who is indisputably gracious, but let's face it, our National Anthem is a disgrace. Give me the Italian one any time over this dismal dirge. Even when belted out by the lads of the Sheffield Wednesday band at England football games it has all the rousing appeal of nineteenth-century funeral processional music. We might as well don widows' weeds and drape ourselves in bits of jet as try to get enthused by this tired old thing. *Rule Britannia*, maybe, or even the over-exposed and much-misunderstood *Jerusalem*. Or a decent bit of Elgar or Parry or even Vaughan Williams. But please God save us from 'God Save the Queen'.

The National Trust

Laudable in aim but too often these days gruesome in reality. Too many shops selling the same chintzy tat; too many tired sandwiches; too many people of a certain age in beige all-weather trousers; too many chatty signs; too much effort unsuccessfully spent trying to 'engage'; too many child-friendly elements, which only serve to alienate the grown-ups. Oh, and too many rules.

See also Dumbing down, Rules, Visitor centres

The Proms

A series of sometimes really quite good performances of classical music, that used to be given solely in the Royal Albert Hall, but which now bizarrely seems to extend to all sorts of content in all sorts of venues. Whatever, every performance, sadly, is marred by the embarrassing behaviour of 'promenaders', the majority of whom, self-evidently, are only there to flaunt their 'amusing' character defects. This tedium is too rarely relieved, sadly, by the onset of their applause a WHOLE MOVEMENT before the end of the piece, which provides a short moment of smugness to those better educated. Whoever said *schadenfreude* is a bad thing...?

See also Concert-goers who start conducting

The Royal Family

An extended family group of supposedly blue-blooded people, notable for its propensity to propagate within the confines of its clan and for an unhealthy obsession with matters equestrian. One or two of the family members display virtues which can be broadly approved, as well as a dedication to their role which is to be applauded. But most seem to waft about in a fairly useless fashion, doing little of perceived value whatsoever – but doing it with a sense of entitlement and self-regard that is staggering. AND WE PAY TOWARDS IT.

It is usual for unenthusiastic defenders of this system to resort to the lame proposition that all the credible alternatives to being lorded over by people who have inherited their exalted positions are worse/no better, so let's just stick to what we have. On that basis, we might as well let the Post Office run the nation's phone network. I don't think so: I can remember when you literally had to bribe telephone engineers to install a line – and still wait six weeks for it. I rest my case.

See also The National Anthem

The wrong kind of snow/rain/leaves/sun etc.

A metaphysical concept developed at awaydays convened by rail operators in order to come up with ever-more inventive reasons for train delays. The Victorians didn't have this problem, apparently, because their trains were heavier (sub excuse #73 in the lexicon of abject excuses for failure). Anyway, the point is that neither railway lines nor the trains that use them can cope with anything that is 10 per cent off an optimum condition for travel, i.e. a temperature of 22 degrees, slightly heavier rain than drizzle, the sort of leaf fall that might be occasioned by a force 2-3 on the Beaufort Scale, or any snow beyond the lightest of flurries (for a more detailed explanation please see the snowflake graphics in sub excuse #149 for more detail).

Theme parks

Without exception, vile, contrived and pointless, unless as a means of emptying more civilised recreational destinations of hordes of people you'd rather avoid.

'There's a good service on all Underground lines'

Oh well done! What do you expect – genuflection at the top of the escalator? Please save the use of your PA system for something actually worthwhile, such as the news that well, actually, sad to relate, but there ISN'T a good service on all Underground lines.

See also Public transport announcements

Things that were once effective but no longer are

After millennia of progress, and in the same way that sleeping policemen and traffic-calming measures have pointlessly reduced the average speed in which we traverse the country, so products that were once efficacious have either been banned or de-tuned to such an extent that the human condition is immeasurably poorer as a result. I'm not just talking about chemistry sets – with their thrilling capacity for creating lethal potions and explosives – but such other essentials as mothballs, patio cleaner, weedkiller and slam-door commuter trains. Thank God that absinthe is now once again freely available, so at least there is something life-threatening we can still quietly enjoy in the privacy of our own homes.

See also Low-energy light bulbs, Sleeping policemen

Ticket machines

See also All ticket machines

Toilet flushes

Bring back Thomas Crapper and his simple, solid, foolproof device for flushing the loo, and let's abandon all these new-fangled devices that work intermittently or half-heartedly, or both. This is not an area where occasional efficacy is an acceptable option, however cool-looking the design: if you need to flush the loo, you don't want the option of a button that intimates 'Press here if you're mildly interested in the possibility of disposing of the contents of the toilet'. And whereas the averagely competent DIYer could replace any parts of a conventional flush that were worn out, it takes a highly qualified technician with a bagful of diplomas to tackle one of the newer formats, which lends a whole new meaning to the phrase 'toilet training'.

See also Taps/plugs that don't work

Too-frequent firework displays

Guy Fawkes night: good. Bastille Day: good. Diwali: good. Firework displays on almost all other occasions are to be deplored as an unnecessary indulgence (unless you're a Maltese, in whose case tradition has it that they should be held on an almost daily basis. Something to do with the Knights Templar, no doubt). People get blasé and dissatisfied; the dogs are frightened; and local authorities have to go cap-in-hand to their ratepayers seeking a bailout because what should have been spent, for example, on care for the elderly has gone up in smoke.

Tourists

A blight on all once-worth-visiting destinations the world over. Too many people, too badly dressed, too noisy, travelling too far and too often, and exhibiting too little taste. On that note I remember reading recently that more of them go to the shopping malls and out-of-town discount centres of Italy than the museums, but that doesn't stop them clogging up the airports, bars and restaurants of Venice, Rome and Florence. I blame that Thomas Cook, but if more of his unwitting modern-day disciples stuck to his temperance ideals and original itinerary – which didn't extend beyond the borders of Leicestershire – then Stansted, Faro, Malaga and East Midlands airports might not have become the hell-holes they regrettably now are. And there'd still be standing room on the Ponte Vecchio.

T-shirts with desperately unfunny slogans

You'd like to think that the seedy-looking chap wearing a pale-coloured T-shirt tightly stretched over his muffin-top bearing the inscription 'SEX GOD' has a strong sense of irony. But you'd be wrong. It's just crass, in the same way that things like fake bloodstains, the monogram FCUK, and the question 'DO MY NIPPLES OFFEND YOU?' are.

Like those tourists wearing 'Cambridge University' T-shirts who've almost certainly never got beyond kindergarten in their home country, or people who weren't conceived until decades after the original performance of *Dark Side of the Moon* wearing facsimile Pink Floyd tour tops.

And why is the humour always on a par with the cheaper kind of birthday card? 'I'M A VIRGIN (This is an old T-shirt)' is typical. Plus, if you're French, you'll almost certainly be wearing a T-shirt which you think is sooo cool but actually just bears three random English words strung together by a backstreet manufacturer in Zhengzhou who knows no better: I'll bet someone, somewhere in France is convinced that the phrase 'MY LOVELY STRAWBERRY PANTIES', for example, is the height of Brit-chic and is mystified by the old-fashioned looks she receives from every passing Englishman.

Trunki

Who HASN'T fallen over one of these at an airport? Lethal.

Twitter

Have you, like me, noticed how the denizens of the so-called civilised world seemed to rub along moderately well (admittedly with a few bumps in the road) before the advent of Twitter a dozen or so years ago? David Cameron never spoke truer than when he memorably once said, 'too many tweets might make a twat', though I might take issue with the word 'might' in that context. Who ARE all these people, so convinced that we want to hear their condensed view on anything and everything? Apparently, there are now well over 300 million of them, all itching to tweet us, for example, the contents of their breakfast, their in-tray or their mind. All of which often turn out to be equally uninteresting to anyone with half a brain, and 99 per cent of which would probably be rescinded if the tweeter gave a nanosecond's thought (or a night's sleep) before pressing Send.

Donald Trump – I rest my case.

I mean – how likely IS it that genuinely significant figures like Churchill or Roosevelt would have resorted to tweeting? Mind you, that double-dealing, serially ungrateful De Gaulle might well have done, with pithy words like 'non' being pretty much tailor-made for the medium. I find myself surprised that no one has yet obtained a generous grant for the purpose of revisiting history to imagine what kind of tweets celebrities from the past would have sent (though someone at an anonymous college in some far-flung corner of the States probably already has). My starter for ten might be Lord Kitchener: 'Your country needs you. #westernfrontlotstodo #thehunathoroughlynastytype #packupyourtroublesinyouroldkitbag'.

Over to you.

See also Quasi-famous 'lifestyle' bloggers, Virtue-signalling, Woke

U

Uggs

Ugh. A bit like the name implies. Was this self-conscious irony, do you suppose, or is the close relationship with 'ugly' just one of those happy coincidences that brightens one's day?

Unnecessary cushions

What is it with this fetish for piling up cushions in serried ranks on beds and sofas, especially in hotels, that make it impossible to sit/lie down in the way nature intended? Who started this

bizarre trend – and why? I've a sneaking feeling it was that Anouska Hempel (maybe she had a very bad back). Am I the only person who, on arriving in such a hotel room, makes it my first duty to throw them all on the floor?

And while I'm on the subject, who came up with that nasty strip of heavy material that hotels increasingly drape along the foot of the bed, and that also ends up in a pile on the floor? Does it have a name – never mind purpose?

See also Hotel room-keys that don't work

Unnecessary signs

'Beware. Pickpockets operate in this area.' Look – if you know that, why not just remove the pickpockets, and then you can remove the sign. Only a few million left to go, then. If signs have the potential for amusement (e.g. 'Slippery when wet') then a few could be left dotted about as a morale-booster. Similarly, if they've been amusingly defaced (in the corner of our garden once stood a sign announcing Ash Grove, to which one of our offspring inventively added an H prefix...leading even more amusingly – in our eyes – to the sight of a local worthy scrubbing away at half-inch thick indelible black ink for the best part of a Saturday morning), they could be left to gently fade away, before ideally being removed altogether.

Why is it, though, that ancient signs were so much more satisfactory than those in evidence in our era? 'Please do not distract the driver whilst the bus is in motion' was an early favourite of mine, with its lovely sentence formation and civil tone. 'Kindly refrain from smoking' was another – and, before my time, 'Careless talk costs lives'. I would happily see half a penny added to my income tax if it would help pay for a host of signs warning people that 'careless grammar costs sanity'. Let's hope someone from the Treasury is reading.

If only they all had the charm of '*Défense de marcher sur les pelouses*'. Say that *sotto voce* and slowly, in the manner of the girl singer from Nouvelle Vague and you could be forgiven for thinking that the speaker is making some sort of erotic injunction to you.

Moving on swiftly as we must: self-evidently the only good road sign is the destricting one that permits you to drive at a decent speed, viz. 60 or 70 mph. All others are of questionable use, especially when there's a cluster going from 30 mph to 50 mph to 40 mph and back to 30 mph within a quarter of a mile. I read somewhere that the number of road signs has doubled in the past twenty years: wouldn't our money have been better spent on refilling all those blasted potholes (*see* potholes) and permit us to use a modicum of common sense?

The same applies to our rail system, in spades. To take one example: the arrivals board which tells you that the 0957 is On Time, when you can see perfectly clearly that the same sign is giving the time as 1001 and on looking down roughly two miles of straight rail-track you can see no sign of the train's impending arrival. That means it will be at least 1007, i.e. ten minutes late. Pray – what, in that context, does the phrase 'On Time' mean? Answers on a postcard please.

And instances of unnecessary signs abound throughout everyday life. 'Please turn these taps gently' advised one I saw in some public conveniences. Poor things – what's wrong them? 'This door is alarmed' said another: why, what's frightened it? 'Caution. Hot water' said the sign above the hot tap. Well thank goodness for that – but why feel the need to inform me?

See also Nannying

Unnecessary streetlights

What's wrong with a bit of proper darkness of a night-time? The world isn't chock-full of muggers, street pads and ne'er-do-wells, after all. If you've ever seen an image of the northern hemisphere from space, or even flown over somewhere like India at night, you'll know what I'm getting at: gazillions of white or sodium lamps illuminating god-knows-what all night long. Can't they be turned down or off…or even half of them off? It's only when you're doing something like crossing Biscay in pitch darkness that you appreciate what we're missing – and why owls are so pissed off with life.

And while I'm on the subject – why are so many office blocks (including government ones) brilliantly lit all night long? It can't all be just for the benefit of Mrs Mop and her fellow scrubbers or a host of hot-deskers. And why do shops have the heating turned up high and the doors open all day long in winter? And vice versa in summer. Oh – and why are train heaters so often full on when the outside temperature is in the 30s but hors de combat in midwinter? That'll be Mr Sod and his incongruous Law at work, for sure.

Unwanted participating in the listening experience of others

Even if you're listening to one of Beethoven's late string quartets or the masterwork that is Dire Straits' *Money for Nothing*, I'd really rather make my own decision about whether I want to hear it right now. Leaking from your headphones. Tskkk tutta tutta tuta tsk tsk tsk…on and on…ad bloody nauseam.

If you choose not to invest in noise-reduction technology at least do us all a favour and TURN THE DAMN THING

DOWN! And what about those 'hot hatches' where the exhaust manifold seems to have been replaced with a boom box, and you're stuck next to them in a traffic jam for what seems like hours? Couldn't you at least close the effing windows?! Ooomp puppa oomp oomp oomp oomp OOOOMPP! Kindly confine your garage music to the garage and not out on the open road.

USBs

I know I'm not the first to draw attention to this syndrome, but it is surely one of the most hideous continuing experiences of this, or any other, age. How can it be, given that statistically one has a 50:50 chance of shoving the USB into its slot the right way up, that 98.3 per cent of the time, one tries to ram it in the wrong way up first time? What's that about?! Am I alone in thinking that the two little – slightly different in appearance – holes on either side of the USB should be a bit of a giveaway? Take it from me – they're not. I estimate that if I have this experience five times a day, 365 days a year, I've already wasted 18 250 minutes engaged in this futile activity. That's TWENTY DAYS OF MY WAKING LIFE!

Surely all those no doubt hardworking chaps at the USB Implementers Forum (yes, there really IS such a thing) could use a tiny age of their working day to devise a simple visual clue to make clear which way up their Universal Serial Bus (don't ask me, I'm merely the reporter here) should be inserted, therefore preventing so much unnecessary angst. It's the sort of thing Barnes Wallis would surely have come up with over a cup of tea whilst he was still stirring his sugar.

See also Bicycle wheels

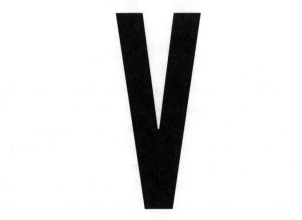

Vaping

It is self-evidently no coincidence that just about the nearest word to vaping, that peculiar newish habit increasingly encouraged by 'big tobacco', is vapid. Can there be any human activity more lacking in character or dignity than daintily sucking on a small, pricey plastic device and exhaling noxious fruit-flavoured fumes, to the detriment of everyone within a 100-metre radius? If you CANNOT resist the joy of sucking and blowing foul-smelling smoke over a horde of people, why not go the whole hog and invest in a decent briar and a pouch of 'old goatherd's fetid sock fungus' or some such – that way, at least you're doing something vaguely meaningful and interesting (I speak from no little experience, as it happens). Or maybe a fatboy cigar that's been rolled on the inner thigh of an elderly Cuban matron and still retains some of the inevitable pungency that the action brings about. For goodness' sake, whoever said, in the hope of increasing their circle of admirers, 'Hey, let's do something supercool – let's go behind the pav for a sneaky vape'? I rest my case.

Velour tracksuits

Yuk. And always on the wrong people, for a start. And REALLY wrong when travelling. 'Juicy Lucy', or whatever the brand is, may sound appetising, but the actuality is seldom pleasing, with the wearer looking for all the world as though they should be curled up on a sofa with a tin of Quality Street rather than traipsing through Passport Control with their curves too obviously in all the wrong places.

Very white trainers

Acceptable on the tennis court or in the gym, for example, but never elsewhere – especially with a suit, dark-coloured or otherwise. Generally speaking, it is axiomatic that the sportier the look, the more corpulent the owner, and I suspect that there is a direct inverse correlation between actual sporting achievement and the number of logos/stripes/flashes on the sports clothing of someone not at that moment engaged in athletic activity.

See also Velour tracksuits

VIP areas

An oxymoronic concept, in that no such thing as a genuine VIP would ever be seen dead in something called a VIP area. This inherent contradiction is manifest in the types of people you always see lurking in such places, guzzling bottles of nondescript champagne at £200 a pop (almost literally). And why do airports boast VIP lounges – and why are they called that? I used to assume they were holding areas for visiting dictators and their ghastly entourages, but I now know that they are repositories for a collection of furniture that looks as if it has been liberated from particularly downmarket old people's homes, and in which escapees from the adjacent shopping malls skulk clutching their free whisky and cokes.

See also Doormen, Red ropes outside wannabe in-demand venues

Virtue-signalling

Surely neo-oxymoronic. Actually, no. Forget the neo. Virtue is indisputably a good thing, but somewhat less so when flagged so obviously. Others should be allowed to judge whether what you're doing/saying is virtuous without calling attention to it yourself, which instantly demeans it. Let's face it – virtue-signalling amounts to little more than jumping on a bandwagon in the hope of making oneself look good or redeeming a public image battered by some misdemeanour, like all those Z-list celebs preening themselves in some godforsaken refugee camp in the arse-end of nowhere. What it actually screams is...me, me ME!

See also Prolonged poppy-wearing, Quasi-famous 'lifestyle' bloggers, Red Nose Day, Twitter

Visitor centres

Oh dear. Let me just wander around Stonehenge etc. and work it out all by myself. Please spare me the naff reconstructions, dioramas, extraneous items and the BLOODY SHOP with its gingham, lavender-scented tat. Oh, and the caff with the overdone baked potatoes and the sort-of-chilli with baked beans, for God's sake, and a sprinkling of grated cheddar. Followed by a milky coffee. WHY?!

See also The National Trust

Visual clichés

The rot started with the Athena tennis girl scratching her bottom, a superb image in its own right but hopelessly overused, rather like the 'Keep Calm...' series of ripoffs. The Bridge of Sighs; Botticelli's *Venus*; almost every Renaissance rendition of the Virgin Mary in the context of Christmas cards; the *Mona Lisa*; those pointy fingers with the sparks between them; the hammock stretched between two palm trees bending towards each other on a white sand beach against an azure sea and sky; commuters walking across Waterloo Bridge...the trouble is, the internet has made it so much easier for images like these to be freely downloaded and used as a lazy shortcut to illustrate stereotypical articles – but must they ALWAYS be the same half-dozen pics?

On which note, why is it always teenage girls jumping for joy on receipt of their A-level results: do boys only get crap grades these days? And do real students who've just graduated really throw their mortarboards in the air, as if they were cadets at West Point? And it now seems that even graduands of playschool don mortar boards and hold prom parties to mark their imminent arrival at Year 1 of the local primary school, to be featured prominently in next week's paper...and next year's, ad bloody nauseam.

See also Clichés, 'Keep calm and...'

W

Waiting staff who won't catch your eye

Many years ago, at a restaurant in Kensington, we made the schoolboy error after dinner of asking for the bill. Eight times. After half an hour of entreaties, we decided to ask for our coats instead, and on receipt of these, said our goodbyes and went on our way, leaving the bill unpaid. They seemed utterly at a loss to see my point of view when I received a phonecall not long after to tell me that I hadn't paid, and I explained in excruciating detail how much I'd wanted to and how hard I'd tried.

HOW MANY TIMES have you suffered the same experience? What IS it with these people? You arrive at a restaurant, are shown to your table, and then spend half an hour in the vain attempt of attracting a waiter's attention in the forlorn hope of getting your hands on the menu. But he's preoccupied with drifting aimlessly about, resting his eyes on anything – everything (even though he's seen it all a thousand times!) – but the pleading looks of one of only three tables that are occupied out of a dozen. Is there a special module at catering college ('Best practice in disappointing your customers', maybe), in which you have to attain 100 per cent to be sure of getting a Starred First in Waitering? And why is it an immutable law that you will have to ask thirteen times for a carafe of water, and that when it eventually arrives you will be expected to swig from the neck of the bottle since the concept of water glasses in addition to wine glasses is clearly an eccentricity too far.

It's the same with barmen, obviously. Working at a student bar back in the day we prided ourselves in never missing a trick, getting the serving priorities right in terms of first come, first served, taking the money AND ensuring no one died needlessly of thirst for want of being served in a timely fashion. Hey, it's hardly rocket science, is it? So why, then, do so many bar staff fail to notice me at all (am I THAT unimpressive?), or if they do, assume you came after the two round-buying blokes who are in the process of ordering a dozen complicated drinks (probably including multi-ingredient alcohol-free cocktails), but who actually arrived AFTER you, and to whom it then comes as a complete surprise that they're expected to pay. At which point, the fumbling for wallets adds so much time, that you start to despair and realise the babysitter only has half an hour to go before she needs to be relieved, so to speak.

W*nkers

See also Bankers, Doormen, Middle managers, Ministry of Defence

Warning labels

It is axiomatic that risk assessments are only ever carried out when there is an infinitesimally small chance of anything significantly bad actually happening. 'Caution. If this water is too hot, kindly inform the management.' Oh for God's sake – just turn the f*cking tap off and run cold water over your fingers. 'Slippery when wet'. Yes, of course it will be – it has been ever since rain was invented, and the early hominids tiptoed carefully across the tundra, almost certainly more aware of their environment than we seem to be after almost six million years of progress. 'Investments may go down in value…': has nobody ever heard of the Great Depression?

There's nothing wrong with a bit of risk in life, so do we really need metaphorically to be hit over the head with absurd warnings of imminent peril when, for example, we buy a small box of fireworks, an appliance with a plug attached, a trampoline or a lilo? (We KNOW it's not a life-saving device). If in the unlikely event of buying a military-grade rocket-launcher it might be an idea to be warned of the risk of holding it the wrong way round. And no doubt even the most alert of dwarves should be advised about the things that might go wrong when fired from a cannon. But a keener sense of perspective would allow the rest of us to get on with everyday life without continually being adjured to look to our wellbeing and be aware of the risks contingent on just about every petty action we take.

See also Health & Safety, Nannying, Public transport announcements

Weather forecasts that contain nothing of any use

Have you noticed how TV weather forecasts almost imperceptibly have become in effect vehicles for streams of consciousness and limp attempts at humour on the part of most of the presenters. Simultaneously, so-called clever graphics call attention to themselves rather than conveying anything of value. For some welcome clarity, bring back Bill Giles with a few well-chosen words and stick-on symbols (and yes, for old time's sake let's have a couple of them fall off mid-presentation). And please – no mention of how the weather's been TODAY (we already know that, you numpties); 'mist and murk' (why are they ALWAYS paired?); and 'spits and spots' (ditto). And you know what you can do with your 'values', 'met office warnings' and damn-fool 'oktas'! That's right – stick 'em where the sun don't shine! Just tell us... is it going to be hot/cold, dry/wet, calm/windy, clear/foggy, later today and tomorrow? Er, that's it. Thanks.

See also Clichés

'We must do lunch sometime'

Dread words, invariably pronounced with an air of utter sincerity that totally belies the underlying truth: YOU'RE NEVER GOING TO MEET UP AGAIN…YOU BOTH KNOW IT…SO PLEASE, SPARE US THE PLATITUDES. It's that 'sometime' that's the giveaway, with its optimistic impression of imminence undermined by a strong sense of unreality. Why not just say, 'I'm glad we met, even if we are unlikely ever to do so again because I just cannot be arsed to make the effort to improve my already-excellent social life'?

And in the unlikely event that a date arising from this sort of encounter is eventually made, you will be completely unsurprised when it gets cancelled at the last minute, with an apology that manages to sound just as sincere as the original comment but still communicate complete unbelievability.

So next time in the course of saying your goodbyes, if someone should pronounce, 'We must do lunch sometime?' why don't you just reply sweetly, 'Oh really – why?' and watch the expression on their face. It might not make you popular but it'll be a lot of fun.

'We will shortly be landing into…'

No, we won't. Let's get this right. 'We will shortly be landing AT…'

I suppose it is unfortunately conceivable that if things go wrong we might shortly find ourselves landing INTO the Everglades swamps rather than Miami International Airport, for example. Or the Atlantic. But in the case of Heathrow etc., there IS no into.

See also Station stop

Wet wipes

If they weren't needed by previous generations, why are they needed now? As it is so easy to combine, for example, a small towel/napkin/tissue with some spittle/water/lotion (if you must) and use it to obtain the desired result, why resort to pre-moistened products that are only going to contribute to the 'fatbergs' clogging the world's sewers and even apparently reshaping the bed of the Thames as it wends its way across London through a morass of modern man's detritus.

What the critics say

One should obviously never trust any of those phrases that adorn posters promoting films or theatrical productions, because few if any convey the sense that the critic intended. You know the kind of thing: 'I'd like to say that this was a superb performance but in all honesty it was one of the most abject displays I've had the misfortune to sit through in two decades of reviewing plays' becomes simply '...this was a superb performance...'. There should be an OFWAT or OFCOM-type body to oversee the use of reviewers' words in cinema/theatre/book publicity and issue public corrections if necessary. Wouldn't you love it if the promoter were forced to issue a new set of ads stating in large bold type, 'One of the most abject displays I've ever had the misfortune to sit through'?! I for one would LOVE to work for a quango called something like OFTWAT, the Office for Testing Words About Theatres – just think of the fun you could have! 'A revelation!', for example, would become 'Plumbs the depths of awfulness' from a sentence that reads, 'A revelation! I cannot believe that anything on the London stage could manage in this day and age quite so thoroughly to plumb the depths of awfulness.' Have fun inventing your own double-edged reviews – and while you're at it, why not come up with some fun quango acronyms too?

Wheelie luggage that hasn't mastered the master-slave relationship

Presumably the inventor of the wheelie bag (do you think he walked oddly and therefore invented the wheelie bag to complement his gait?) intended for it to be a small way of making the traveller's life slightly easier. That is to say, the wheelie bag was conceived to be our servant, not our master. Why is it, then, that so many take on the dominant role? If, for example, you don't step off a kerb at a precise right-angle (a bit like sailing across the English Channel shipping lanes), it can be guaranteed that your wheelie bag will protest, and throw all sorts of absurd contortions, just to make a point. All four wheels, of course, will have their own idea about the desired direction of travel, which in the end means you go nowhere until you've given the bag a stern talking-to and (temporarily) reasserted your natural authority over it. That button you're supposed to press to make the handle go up and down is almost certain to work when IT wants – not when YOU want, just for the hell of it. Put one item too many in the zip-up front pocket and you can be sure that as soon as you turn your back, the damn thing will effect a dramatic falling-over. Drama queen. Items of luggage should know their place in the pecking order, which I assure you Mr Samsonite, is nowhere near the top.

See also Trunki

'Where's the bathroom?'

A perfectly reasonable question if you're a guest in someone's house, need a wash, and the location of the bathroom for your use isn't immediately obvious. Less so when you're asking a waiter the way to the WC, although I understand that a certain type of American doesn't get the distinction. They must be very disappointed when they eventually make their way down a dingy flight of stairs to discover that the pub 'bathroom' only contains a stainless steel trough.

'Will you do this for me please?'

Said in a simpering voice by (e.g.) an air hostess requesting one to put away one's tray table. False-sounding and unnecessarily wordy, suggesting extreme neediness on the part of the speaker. 'Please stow away your table' would be an improvement and is all that is required.

See also Simpering

Wine descriptions

Just tell me the name, the grape type(s), the year, the country of origin and the strength. Don't give me all that guff about hints of shoe polish, nuttiness, fresh laundry, school lavatories etc. We all know it's b*llocks. After all, the bottle-shape and the colour alone should tell most people almost all they need to know, and if I choose to have a decent Amarone with my baked cod that's my business: I don't need some supermarket under-manager telling me that its only role in life is to wash down a *bistecca alla Fiorentina*.

See also merlot

Wobbly tables in restaurants

Please tell me: if your dining table at home never wobbles, why does every other table in every other restaurant in every other country do so?

I've lost count of the number of times that I've messed around with business cards, coasters, credit cards, menus, discarded bread rolls, unwanted paperbacks etc. in an attempt to make all four legs sit squarely on the floor. As a corollary of this, it is an observed irony that the customer will be considerably more proficient at this than the waiting staff, who, after all, must have had so much practice.

Woke

Like 'gay', 'woke' is a word whose original meaning has been subverted, which in itself is intensely irritating. So, for example, even if one wanted to, it is no longer possible to state, 'I was asleep, and then I woke before brushing my teeth' without sowing seeds of confusion in the listener. Much more annoying, obviously, is the meaning it has taken on, with its associations of virtue-signalling and cloying social awareness. I mean – shouldn't all of these people have been just a bit awake in the first place, without their social conscience having to be triggered by some extraneous event or self-regarding tweet? Can they all really only just have 'awoken' to the fact that the world is riddled with injustices and prejudices and now need a word to announce that fact to the world? I don't think early social campaigners like Wilberforce, Fawcett and even Gladstone (though his interest in ladies of the street has always seemed a little questionable) needed a badge to denote their state of wakefulness and nor should the lesser mortals of the Academy of Motion Picture, Arts & Sciences – although given the role of the casting couch in many of their lives maybe anything describing their degree of arousal is only to be expected.

See also Absurd beards, Twitter, Virtue-signalling

X-rays

See also airport security

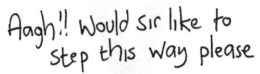

Y

Young people who can only communicate by shouting

Yes, yes – we know you can text too…and we know you're mostly plugged into substantial earphones reminiscent of a special operations operative in occupied France…but why do you all have to SHOUT even when you're having that rare thing, a conversation? All at the same time? About NOTHING?! You can't ALL have been doing voice projection in drama school that week and been told to practise method acting non-stop…

Look, I'd mind less – though not much – if it were even vaguely interesting, but the shenanigans of Tracey in the Lower Sixth aren't top of my list of intriguing eavesdropping. Though come to think of it, there are more tedious topics.

Zeitgeist

Word currently much overused, especially by those who haven't Wthat they are in tune with the spirit of the age and have more gravitas than the man on the Clapham omnibus.

Acknowledgements

My thanks first of all to everyone out there who unwittingly provided inspiration for this ground-breaking work. I would say, you know who you are – but I bet you don't.

A more proper thank you to my wife Philippa who, as will be self-evident, has a lot with which to put up. On the other hand (see 'reloading the dishwasher for no good reason' for instance), she largely brings it on herself. Obvs.

Then there's Nigel Rodgers, a constant friend of almost fifty years' standing, who encouraged me, and also introduced Tom Cull, who became my literary agent (THERE'S posh!) and therefore merits a special mention.

There are of course other sources of inspiration too numerous to mention, so it would be invidious of me to try. But unlike the unconscious contributors mentioned above – you almost certainly know who you are.

Find out more about RedDoor
Press and sign up to our
newsletter to hear about our
latest releases, author events,
exciting **competitions**
and more at

reddoorpress.co.uk

YOU CAN ALSO FOLLOW US:

 @RedDoorBooks

 Facebook.com/RedDoorPress

 @RedDoorBooks